# GUID

C000001816

January–April 2018

Commissioned by **David Spriggs** | Edited by **Lisa Cherrett**

**The Bible Reading Fellowship**
15 The Chambers, Vineyard
Abingdon OX14 3FE
brf.org.uk

The Bible Reading Fellowship (BRF) is a Registered Charity (233280)

ISBN 978 0 85746 551 1

Distributed in Australia by:
MediaCom Education Inc, PO Box 610, Unley, SA 5061
Tel: 1 800 811 311 | admin@mediacom.org.au

Distributed in New Zealand by:
Scripture Union Wholesale, PO Box 760, Wellington
Tel: 04 385 0421 | suwholesale@clear.net.nz

**Acknowledgements**
The New Revised Standard Version of the Bible, Anglicised Edition, copyright © 1989,
1995 by the Division of Christian Education of the National Council of the Churches of
Christ in the USA. Used by permission. All rights reserved.

The Holy Bible, New International Version, Anglicised edition, copyright © 1979,
1984, 2011 by Biblica. Used by permission of Hodder & Stoughton Publishers, an
Hachette UK company. All rights reserved. 'NIV' is a registered trademark of Biblica.
UK trademark number 1448790.

Printed by Gutenberg Press, Tarxien, Malta

# Suggestions for using *Guidelines*

Set aside a regular time and place, if possible, when you can read and pray undisturbed. Before you begin, take time to be still and, if you find it helpful, use the BRF Prayer on page 6.

In *Guidelines*, the introductory section provides context for the passages or themes to be studied, while the units of comment can be used daily, weekly, or whatever best fits your timetable. You will need a Bible (more than one if you want to compare different translations) as Bible passages are not included. At the end of each week is a 'Guidelines' section, offering further thoughts about, or practical application of what you have been studying.

Occasionally, you may read something in *Guidelines* that you find particularly challenging, even uncomfortable. This is inevitable in a series of notes which draws on a wide spectrum of contributors, and doesn't believe in ducking difficult issues. Indeed, we believe that *Guidelines* readers much prefer thought-provoking material to a bland diet that only confirms what they already think.

If you do disagree with a contributor, you may find it helpful to go through these three steps. First, think about why you feel uncomfortable. Perhaps this is an idea that is new to you, or you are not happy at the way something has been expressed. Or there may be something more substantial – you may feel that the writer is guilty of sweeping generalisation, factual error, theological or ethical misjudgment. Second, pray that God would use this disagreement to teach you more about his word and about yourself. Third, think about what you will do as a result of the disagreement. You might resolve to find out more about the issue, or write to the contributor or the editors of *Guidelines*.

To send feedback, you may email **enquiries@brf.org.uk** or write to BRF at the address shown opposite. You can also tweet to **@brfonline**, using the hashtag **#brfconnect**.

3

# Writers in this issue

**David Spriggs** provides occasional consultancy services for Bible Society, but his main role is as a Baptist minister again. He has recently been appointed as a part-time minister with the Friar Lane and Braunstone Baptist Church, Leicester.

**Steve Motyer** loves the quest for understanding – and the Bible is central to this quest. His life as a carer helps with this, as does 30 years of teaching New Testament and Counselling at London School of Theology.

**Antony Billington** is Head of Theology at the London Institute for Contemporary Christianity, having formerly taught hermeneutics and biblical theology at London School of Theology.

**Hugh Williamson** was the Regius Professor of Hebrew at Oxford University until he retired in 2014. He has written extensively on the books of Chronicles, Ezra and Nehemiah, and on Isaiah.

**Tim Davy** teaches Biblical Studies and Mission at Redcliffe College in Gloucester. His PhD was on a missional reading of Job, and he is particularly interested in the missional interpretation of the Bible.

**David Beresford** is currently the Director of Catholic Bible School and, with his wife Sarah, has a passion for storytelling and bringing the Bible to life. He has been actively engaged in ministry for over 25 years.

**David Dewey** is a Baptist minister now serving both Baptist and Anglican communities in South Yorkshire. Alongside helping people engage with scripture, his interests include Bible translation and interpretation.

**David Cohen** is the Head of Biblical Studies at Vose Seminary in Perth Australia. He completed doctoral research on the efficacy of lament psalms several years ago and continues to write and lecture on this topic and others.

**Ian Paul** is Associate Minister at St Nic's Nottingham, and Honorary Assistant Professor at the University of Nottingham, as well as Managing Editor at Grove Books in Cambridge. He blogs at **www.psephizo.com**.

In his retirement, **Derek Tidball** continues to be very active in pastoring, writing and theological education. His most recent book is *Called by God* (BRF, 2017). He is married to Dianne and lives in Leicester.

**Anthony Thacker** is Minister at Burbage Congregational Church, and was Baptist Minister in Treforest, Oadby, Billesdon and Hinckley. His interests include musical composition, systematic theology, history and science fiction.

# David Spriggs writes...

Mark begins his Gospel with a resounding note – 'The beginning of the good news of Jesus Christ, the Son of God'. Steve Motyer will be taking us through the first eight chapters of Mark throughout this year. Offering us a vital window on to and into the story of Jesus, Steve will help us see Jesus with new vitality. I am sure that, like me, you will find many fresh insights as he shares with us from his rich knowledge and spirituality.

Appropriately, in the first two weeks of this year we explore some of the many new beginnings in the Bible, including creation, Passover, the incarnation and the 'new creation'. As we reflect on the significance of God's new starts, these can enrich our spiritual engagement with this New Year.

In this New Year issue we have four new authors. David Beresford will explore the parables of Jesus to give us insight about growth in God's kingdom. David Cohen and David Dewey are also new, and they join Hugh Williamson in offering us contributions on the Psalms. David Dewey engages with the Passover psalms and their relationship to the last days of Jesus' earthly ministry. David Cohen tackles some psalms of lament. Lament is a strange world, but is vital if our spirituality is to withstand the shocks and challenges of life. Hugh Williamson looks at the psalms which begin and end each of the five 'books' of Psalms. By looking at these structurally situated psalms, Hugh helps us see how we can reread them for our day.

Four familiar authors bring more riches from the Bible into our lives. Antony Billington reflects on biblical insights into our working lives and offers us deep and challenging perspectives on the way many of us spend 25 per cent of our time. Tim Davy focuses on the theme of adoption, and the power of this metaphor in scripture (including its place in the purposes of God).

As we near the resurrection, Ian Paul uses Paul's letters to help us appreciate the rich and far-reaching aspects of Christ's resurrection for our faith.

We live in a universe which is revealed to us as ever-increasing in size, complexity and mystery. Derek Tidball's exposition of Colossians presents us with the vision and impact of a 'cosmic Christ' – God's adequate answer to the messy and mysterious universe depicted. And finally – the fourth new writer is Anthony Thacker. He has a special interest in relating the Christian faith to science fiction. Here he takes some of the profound issues which science fiction uses as its subtext and relates them to biblical insights.

I wish you God's blessing as you discover more of the riches of scripture through this issue, 'asking that you may be filled with the knowledge of God's will' (Colossians 1: 9).

5

# The BRF Prayer

*Almighty God,*
*you have taught us that your word is a lamp for our feet*
*and a light for our path. Help us, and all who prayerfully*
*read your word, to deepen our fellowship with you*
*and with each other through your love.*
*And in so doing may we come to know you more fully,*
*love you more truly, and follow more faithfully*
*in the steps of your son Jesus Christ, who lives and reigns*
*with you and the Holy Spirit, one God for evermore.*
*Amen*

# New beginnings

As we enter this new year, we do so in the company of the Bible. This book recognises and reflects on 'new beginnings'. It does so from the start to the end.

Genesis 1:1 says, 'In the beginning when God created the heavens and the earth...'

And Revelation 21:1 completes the journey: 'Then I saw a new heaven and a new earth.'

This, however, only kick-starts us for another greater new journey: 'And I saw the holy city, the new Jerusalem, coming down out of heaven from God, prepared as a bride adorned for her husband' (Revelation 21:2).

Hence, all of the last 10 billion years plus is only leading us to the time when our lives are truly fulfilled as the bride of Christ.

But the Bible focuses not only on these cosmically significant new beginnings which frame our existence, but also on personal and national ones.

At the beginning of our year, we journey with the Bible as it commemorates, challenges and consoles us. Our prayer could well be that of Moses: 'Now, if I have found favour in your sight, show me your ways, so that I may find favour in your sight... He said, 'My presence will go with you, and I will give you rest' (Numbers 33:13–14).

Quotations are from the New Revised Standard Version.

1–7 January

## 1 A perfect start

**Genesis 1:1–13, 26–31**

Although the Bible begins with the reassurance of God's presence and power, it is in the context of the uncontrolled, unpredictable and unknown: 'The earth was a formless void and darkness covered the face of the deep' (v. 2).

Time that has passed, whether we think only of last year or many years, may have been challenging, chaotic and confused, but at least it is not the unknown any longer. We may still feel haunted by it – disasters that happened to us or our family, or troubles that we, in part or in whole, brought on ourselves – but at least we know what happened and we know we have survived; we know what we have lost and what we have salvaged.

But those haunting words from Genesis frighten us (if we pause and identify with them) because they depict a world without structure, whose depths we cannot fathom and whose dread we cannot see. We are looking into an abyss where we can hear and sense the turbulence but cannot comprehend it, let alone have any confidence that we can manage it. It may seem like an image of our year ahead: 'Then God said, "Let there be light" and there was light' (v. 3).

The chaos is under control, the darkness is dispelled, the panic is quelled, the terror is dissolved, the darkness is annihilated and the fear evaporates. Those few spartan words change everything. It is hard to imagine a greater contrast or such a remarkable change accomplished more economically. The raging, roaring lion roaming outside the tent has become a domesticated cat.

Genesis 1 continues to establish God's supreme control over all the threats to existence. But much more follows. Control is followed by creativity and flourishing. Fear is replaced by reassurance and the familiarity of the world we live in as it emerges in these verses at the command of God (see 1, 4–13). More profoundly still, the same voice which said, 'Let there be light,' affirms his creation: 'And God saw that it was good' (Genesis 1:13).

When Paul looked into the chaos of human existence, he recognised the same calming reality. Nothing 'will be able to separate us from the love of God that is in Christ Jesus our Lord' (Romans 8:39).

These are words that enable us to look into and enter our new year.

## 2  God's unchanging commitment

**Genesis 3:1–12, 17–24**

We have considered the challenge God faced in creating a universe; but the bigger challenge, I suggest, was starting again after 'the fall'. As the Bible presents the developing world, humankind is central to its future as a place of blessing. And humankind has revolted against its creator and so become alienated from the ground of being, distorting reality.

Yes, God has the whole universe and the whole of universal history to consider, and he does not shirk this challenge. Yet his actions portray not violent anger or impersonal intervention but personal tenderness: 'The Lord God made garments of skin for Adam and his wife and clothed them' (v. 21).

Sandwiched between the curses and the banishment from the garden are these tender and amazing words. (It is worth noting in passing that God does not curse Adam and Eve. There are dire consequences for their primordial disobedience but God does not rescind his blessing or substitute a curse for it.)

The creator of the whole universe becomes the personal tailor to Adam and Eve. While they tried to ameliorate their awareness of nakedness by fig leaves (which would soon wilt and die), God provides them with garments made from animal skins which will last a lifetime.

We tend to read the 'nakedness' as sexual awareness of some kind, but biblically it is their nakedness before God rather than each other which is foregrounded (see v. 10). The intimate, trusting relationship before their acts of disobedience was replaced with vulnerability and fear. So God cares for them not simply by making the clothes but by dressing them himself. Thus he begins the long journey for humanity to a changed but renewed relationship with himself.

Our world is the fractured world of chapter 3 not the idyllic world of chapters 1—2. We shall be reminded of this endlessly through our new year. Globally and nationally we shall learn of tragedies and of our apparent inability to truly solve any of the fundamental problems we face. Personally many of us will encounter evil and suffering – this is the space we inhabit and it can seem relentless and impersonal. But God is at work; he is the God of new beginnings and he cares personally and appropriately for us.

# 3 The Passover

**Exodus 12:1–5, 21–32**

So much has happened in the biblical account since Genesis 3 – the devastating flood and the renewal of God's covenant with the earth, and the division of nations and languages at the tower of Babel. Now Israel is in Egypt – no longer favoured because of the brilliance of Joseph, but enslaved. His people's cries reach God and he starts his new work by calling one person, Moses, to return to Egypt and challenge the brutal Pharaoh. At last, Israel is to be set free. This deliverance will be costly but it marks a new beginning that would become the hallmark of God's people: 'This month shall mark for you the beginning of months; it shall be the first month of the year for you' (v. 2).

As we enter our new year we can consider three significant points. Firstly, every new beginning has a long prelude to it. This new year is not entirely new. It is good to consider the mistakes we and others have made which have created our present situation – whether good, bad or, as is normally the case, somewhere in between. But it is even more important to realise that, throughout the long process of our lives, God has been watching over us and has never given up on his redemptive purposes. He never will.

Secondly, we can avoid the trap of thinking everything is always the same and always will be. God does 'make all things new'.

Thirdly, this passage underlines the need to pause and commemorate the 'acts of God'. Over our many years we have experienced many 'new years'. Throughout each year we have celebrated the divine story – Advent, Epiphany, Lent, Holy Week, Easter Day, Pentecost and so on. We can become familiar with the rhythm of the Christian year. Valuable as it is and necessary to have these regular reminders of the story which has sustained the church and shaped our Christian lives, it is equally important to stop ourselves from sustaining a treadmill of lectionary readings. Although there have been 3,000 Passovers, there was a first one. God acted to set his people free. There was also a 'founding one' for us – when we first fully entered into the inheritance we have in Christ. This new year reminds us of our new year: 'So if anyone is in Christ, there is a new creation' (2 Corinthians 5:17).

# 4 Kingship: the first king of Israel

**1 Samuel 9:15–19, 9:25—10:1, 17–26**

Saul's reign marks a new beginning in the political life of Israel and in their relationship with God. Yet the fundamental covenant of God with his people undergirds all these changes (see 10:18).

Nations do change in all kinds of ways. Israel began as a group of tribes and then, through the time of settlement in their promised land, they were territorially dispersed but also learnt to work together to defend each other, under the leadership of judges. Now, partly at least to cope better with aggression from outside of themselves, they move towards a different political structure: monarchy. Initially the changes may not have been very noticeable, but eventually they would be.

The United Kingdom is moving towards a changed relationship with Europe. Arguably this 'Brexit' decision was influenced partly by many years of migration which turned into a fear that the United Kingdom was losing control of its borders and also its identity. Will it be a good or bad outcome?

With Israel's move towards monarchy there is also considerable uncertainty. Sometimes it seems God is happy to grant their request for a king. He is intimately involved in guiding Samuel to encounter Saul and to recognise that he is God's chosen person. In language that is reminiscent of Moses' role in delivering Israel from Egypt, Samuel is told by God to 'anoint [Saul] to be ruler over my people Israel... for I have seen the suffering of my people, because their outcry has come to me' (9:16).

At other times we encounter the sense that in demanding a king Israel were rejecting God (10:19) and disaster would follow.

During times of profound social and political change, we can learn important lessons from this passage. Firstly, it is valid to consider the situation and the changes involved from different, even apparently opposite, viewpoints; there is likely to be deep truth in both.

Secondly, we need to be responsive to the directions God gives us and to act in faith as Samuel did, even when we suspect it will be detrimental to us personally and difficult for our country.

Thirdly, we should play our part in alerting others to the potential pitfalls and in doing anything we can to mitigate them. This is what Samuel is doing in his warnings and his 'rights and duties of kings' manifesto (10:25).

Finally, never forget that through all changes God remains committed to his promises.

# 5 Temple opening

**1 Kings 8:1–21**

The building of Solomon's temple is seen as a very big deal, a highly significant new start for Israel's corporate life. One way to recognise this is by the number of chapters in the Bible devoted to its building; another is the role for good or ill that 'temple' played in biblical and Jewish thought. Within this passage this great importance is underlined by the fact that, while David had longed to build the temple, and God affirmed this was a good intention, the construction was entrusted to Solomon.

The transition from a mobile shrine to a permanent building marked the transition to a new kind of kingship. However, we can note how this passage recognises continuity as well as discontinuity – giving leaders some vital lessons in transitioning.

Firstly, Solomon invites all 'the elders of Israel and all the heads of the tribes' (v. 1). Although the choice of Jerusalem by David as the political centre and now the establishing of the temple as a fixed religious centre would change the power structures in Israel, the old is incorporated.

The ark is treated with the utmost respect. There is no attempt to reject the old and claim only the new is of value. The ark evoked many memories of God's goodness and deliverance, and these are incorporated not buried in the new temple.

The law, given to Moses on Mount Horeb, is recognised as the founding law for the new state. This law applied to king as well as people. It may have been tempting for the temple-building king to produce his own set of laws, so that he was 'above the law', but there is no hint of this.

David is honoured for his part in the opening of the temple. David's longing was to honour God in a way more appropriate for a settled monarchy. This is properly affirmed in Solomon's words. Solomon does not try to take all the credit.

Due recognition is given to the abiding relationship of Israel with God (v. 21 and elsewhere). This is ultimately the most important truth of all to uphold.

This passage provides us with a good model for introducing 'new things' into the life of the church, or indeed for coping with new things which come into our lives. The new is never totally new, even though over time the discontinuities may become more obvious and more impactful.

# 6 The God of new things

**Isaiah 42:5–9; 43:14–21**

The prophets, especially the large books of Isaiah, Jeremiah and Ezekiel, all contain a focus on the 'new things' that God will do. To represent all of this we reflect on Isaiah's thoughts about God's new things: 'Do not remember the former things, or consider the things of old. I am about to do a new thing: now it springs forth, do you not perceive it?' (Isaiah 43:18–19).

Among the new things that are included here is the fact that God is going to redeem his people – to release them from the exile which was the consequence of their disobedience (see Isaiah 40:1–11). In order to do this, a new political process will take place. Never before, until now, at least in recent history, have a people who had been exiled been allowed to return. But God is going to lead his people back from Babylon to Jerusalem under the decree and protection of the Persian ruler, Cyrus (43:14; 44:24—45:1).

To emphasise how radical this new thing was – radical not only in terms of politico-military policy but also in terms of the impact on God's history with Israel – they are told to not remember. This contrasts with many messages of the Old Testament where they are told to 'remember' and 'not forget'.

Yet in the verses that follow there are constant echoes of what God had done before when he took his people from Egypt to the promised land. For instance, the destruction of the pursuing Egyptian army at the 'Red Sea' is echoed in these words: 'Thus says the Lord, who makes a way in the sea, a path in the mighty waters, who brings out chariots and horses, army and warriors, they lie down, they cannot rise, they are extinguished, quenched like a wick' (Isaiah 43:16–17).

The point here, the real point, is not to actually forget the past but to recognise that God can do and does things which are unpredictable from within the normal processes of cause and effect. At the same time, he is the same God, however amazingly 'new' what he does is.

This is supremely exemplified in the ministry and mission of Jesus.

## Guidelines

This week's notes have taken us at lightning speed through the Old Testament as we have journeyed from creation, through the formation of Israel as God's chosen people and on to the promise of a new start for those who were in exile and overwhelmed by their plight.

Reflect on this passage from Isaiah 44: 'Do not fear, for… you are mine. When you pass through the waters, I will be with you: when you walk through the fire you shall not be burned. For I am the Lord your God.'

Look back over last year and consider:

• What did you find most troublesome and distressing in the world situation?

- What surprised you (in a good way) and encouraged you in the world situation?
- What was the most unexpected event, process or decision at a national level? Was this – for you – good, neutral or bad?
- Give thanks for God's promise that 'I am the Lord your God'. Give thanks for his presence through any personal challenges.

Looking forward into the coming year:

- What worries you most about the world situation?
- Pray for those who lead us through the United Nations.
- What do you think are the greatest dangers for us as a nation?
- Pray for the government and the opposition, along with financial and business leaders.
- What threatens your personal life?

Give thanks for the God who says: 'Do not remember the former things, or consider the things of old. I am about to do a new thing: now it springs forth, do you not perceive it?' (Isaiah 43:18).

# 1 New creation

## 2 Corinthians 5

In this second week of 'new beginnings', we will reflect on some of the personal 'new beginnings' we find in the New Testament. But in order to set the scene for this, we begin with Paul's reflections on the Christian's 'new creation'. The immediate context for Paul's astounding claim that 'if anyone is in Christ there is a new creation: everything old has passed away: see, everything has become new' (v. 17) is his own ministry. He is explaining, perhaps even seeking to justify, his own life's work. He and his colleagues are 'ambassadors for Christ' (v. 20). The background for this 'new creation' is, paradoxically, the death of Christ and, with him, the death of everyone else: 'We are convinced that one has died for all: therefore all have died' (v. 14).

All of this background makes Paul's claim about 'new creation' theologically rich and fascinating.

What supports this claim is the language Paul uses and the implications of that. For this is the language of creation – obvious, once it is said, but still astounding. He is drawing a parallel between the transformation of a human being when they join themselves to Christ and the whole creative work of God. One implication of this is that each 'coming to life in Christ' is equivalent to the significance for God of the whole creative process.

This is not an imaginary connection, for Paul is strengthened by his direct link to the God of creation in 2 Corinthians 4:6: 'It is the God who said, "Let light shine out of darkness."' This is a compressed summary of Genesis 1:3–4 using, essentially, the first and last words, '*Let there be light*… God separated the light *from the darkness*' (my emphasis).

But the theological depth of this is further increased by the claim that we are a 'new creation'. We are the first fruits of God's eschatological work when creation will be redeemed and restored – the new heaven and the new earth.

So, as we consider the new beginnings that took place as people first encountered Jesus, and that take place even today, we do well to understand this 'conversion' or 'new birth', or however we choose to describe it, in its full theological depth. We reflect not simply the birth of a star, but of the whole of creation!

# 2  John the Baptist

**Matthew 3:1–17; Luke 3:1–3**

John the Baptist marked a new beginning for his parents, who had been childless and therefore in their culture significantly disadvantaged. He also marked a new beginning for Israel, indicating to those with discernment a new move of God, with many wondering whether he might be the Messiah (Luke 3:15). For a significant number of people, his preaching and baptising led them to a personal new beginning as they committed themselves again to God.

However, our focus is on the new beginnings for John himself. Whereas Matthew introduces John's ministry with, 'In those days John the Baptist appeared' (3:1), Luke goes into more detail. His historical and religious contextualising (see 3:1) sounds as though it is going to be similar to Matthew's account, and then we read: 'The word of God came to John… in the wilderness' (Luke 3:2).

This was the trigger which launched John into his ministry, preparing the way for Jesus. His birth, his rather strange upbringing, his long years in the wilderness, even the expectations which people had of him, were not in themselves enough. It was God's word which launched him. Sometimes hearing and receiving God's word begins our relationship with God, but here it marks the beginning of John's public ministry.

The second new beginning for John comes with his encounter with Jesus. Here it is Matthew who provides us with most detail (3:13–17). John was anticipating someone greater than himself. Verses 11–12 probably indicate that he had in mind the Messiah who would bring God's judgement to the world. Then Jesus turns up – not exactly what he had been describing! But John recognises, through both the familiarity of his cousin and the contrast with his own expectations, that Jesus is 'the one' (3:3). This takes some doing. It equally takes some doing for John to actually perform baptism on Jesus. It all seems so wrong to John. But, we read, 'he consented' (3:15).

As a result, John was privileged to witness the affirmation by God of Jesus as his Son. From now on, John's ministry would be profoundly changed, no longer preparing people for Jesus' coming but pointing people to him (John 1:29–34). John reminds us that whenever we encounter Jesus a profound change takes place, not only in our understanding of the purposes of God but in our lifestyle too.

# 3  New beginnings – for Jesus and his disciples

**Matthew 4:12–25**

Not all new beginnings are welcome. This passage starts with a most significant change for John the Baptist – he has been incarcerated by Herod, resulting ultimately in his vicious murder (Matthew 14:1–12). Just as the death of a monarch marks the end of one era and the beginning of another, so John's imprisonment marks a new beginning for Jesus – the start of his public ministry, with a change of location from Nazareth to Capernaum. Matthew underlines the change by using a quotation from the Old Testament, one which indicates that the change is as significant as the change from darkness to light, from death to life. Matthew's use of this quotation is even more astounding seeing that John's arrest will lead to his death. Indeed ultimately this change will lead to the death of Jesus too. But the heart of the change is not death but life.

The first people who are used to illustrate this change are Simon and

Andrew, and James and John: two pairs of brothers. Although Jesus would later warn that his call could result in the alienation of brother from brother (Matthew 10:21), this call shows that it is not inevitable.

What it also indicates most graphically is that responding to Jesus requires a fundamental change of lifestyle. The ability of Jesus to command a response from these well-established, self-employed fishermen is astounding. His power is even greater than that of a Roman centurion, who while he could command people to drop everything and carry his luggage, could only insist on this temporarily. With Jesus it was a lifetime's change. But the heart of this change is neither compulsion nor a change of career.

The call of Jesus brings its own power. Hearing the words, 'Follow me,' liberates the four young men. There is no trace of reluctance, no anxiety about future provision for their family, no sense of a lost status in their village. Their response is instant: 'Immediately they left' (v. 20).

But neither is Jesus' call, at heart, about losing anything. Two statements make this clear. Firstly, it is actually about repenting, 'for the kingdom of heaven is near' (v. 17). This statement sets the context for the disciples' call, and it provides the context for us to fully follow Jesus into this new year. And the positive is also emphasised: 'I will make you fish for people' (v. 19).

# 4  New birth – Nicodemus

John 3:1–21

Here we have a fascinating conversation between Jesus and one Pharisee – Nicodemus. This is the only private conversation we see between Jesus and a Pharisee. Normally such conversations are public and with a group. Often they are argumentative and sometimes vitriolic. Here there is discussion, but it is deep and we can detect a tinge of humour on both sides.

Although it is possible to hear Nicodemus' question, 'Can one enter a second time into the mother's womb and be born?' as a stupid one, it is more appropriate to hear Nicodemus saying, in effect, 'Come off it, Jesus! Stop pulling my leg!'

The most fundamental issue to consider is the idea of being born 'from above' or 'again'. It is difficult to follow the conversation between Nicodemus and Jesus without grappling with one translation issue. 'Born again' is how Nicodemus hears it – and that is perfectly legitimate – but Jesus means not 'anew' but 'from above' – the Greek can be understood in either or both senses. This 'above' is not primarily a spatial indicator but a dimensional one. Hence 'above' in verse 3 is apparently expanded and explained in verse 5 as 'born of water and Spirit'. Here we need to be careful, however, as in verse 8 the phrase is shortened to 'born of the Spirit'. It is this 'Spirit' birth which represents the dimension of 'above'. Being born of 'water' relates to natural birth out of the amniotic fluid of the womb (see v. 4). So the 'second' or 'new' birth is of a completely different type and origin to our natural birth (see John 1:12–13).

This birth 'of the Spirit' is from God but involves the death of Jesus (vv. 14–15). 'Lifted up' relates here to the physical lifting up of the serpent in the Old Testament story referred to in verses 11–15 (see Numbers 21:4–9), but also to Jesus' death by crucifixion. We have to wait until John 12:27–36 for this to be spelled out. Birth 'from above' also involves the human response of 'believing' in Jesus – but this also is the work of the unpredictable Spirit.

This 'new birth' is profoundly connected with doctrines of salvation and the Holy Spirit. It is also absolutely essential. Would Nicodemus ever experience this 'being born from above'?

# 5 Emmaus (cross and resurrection)

**Luke 24:13–35**

The most fundamental new beginning recorded in the New Testament begins with a death! In this most beautiful of resurrection accounts, we see through the eyes of the two travellers, late on the 'third day', how completely negative that death of Jesus seemed to them.

Jesus had raised great hopes that he was the 'new beginning'; as Cleopas put it, 'the one to redeem Israel' (v. 21). That was the new beginning Jesus' contemporaries longed for. Pharisees tried to keep the law meticulously to hasten the day of its arrival. The zealots tried to initiate it with violence and even martyrdom. Many saw Jesus as 'the one'. But all this seemed to have proved a cruel deceit: 'But *we had hoped* that he was the one to redeem Israel' (v. 21, my emphasis).

All such hopes had been smashed as the religious leaders had ruthlessly and successfully engineered Jesus' death (v. 20). But for God and humanity, this death was the most profound new beginning (see 24:47).

'Jesus of Nazareth' (v. 19) would not only restore the hopes of those who saw in him the redeemer of Israel, but would transcend these hopes – he was to be the redeemer of all nations.

Yet his betrayal and death were not 'accidents of history'; they were not unfortunate incidents on the road to victory that caused minor delays. They were a necessary part of God's plan. This plan was foretold in scripture and is underlined as a fundamental part of God's process for universal redemption: 'Was it not necessary that the Messiah should suffer these things and then enter his glory?' (v. 26).

Jesus' suffering was a divine necessity, but so was the outcome – that he would 'enter his glory'. We should probably see in this phrase the recognition that Jesus' resurrection was the acclamation by God the Father that Jesus is the redeemer. This is mirrored for us in the account of Jesus' transfiguration, where seeing Jesus' glory (Luke 9:22) leads God to the acclamation, 'This is my Son, my chosen one' (Luke 9:35).

The cross, and all that Jesus suffered, is the start – making possible for all people the new beginning of a 'redeemed' life with God. Equally, of course, the resurrection is an intimate and inseparable component of this new beginning. Without that the Messiah could not walk with his broken disciples, restoring their past hope and then extending it beyond their imagination.

# 6 Still more to come

**Revelation 21:1–8; 22:1–7**

This passage is overflowing with newness. There is a 'new heaven and a new earth'; there is the 'holy city, the new Jerusalem'; and climactically there is the divine claim, 'See, I make all things new' (21:1, 2, 5). At the heart of this newness is the dissolution of the breach between heaven and earth. In effect, heaven and earth become one reality, just as Jesus had taught his disciples to pray (see Matthew 6:9–10).

This final vision seeks to depict what overcoming the difference between heaven and earth is like: 'See, the home of God is among mortals. He will dwell with them; they will be his peoples, and God himself will be with them' (Revelation 21:3).

At the heart of this newness is the obvious presence of God among his peoples. Although the plural 'peoples' is preferred by the NRSV, it also notes the alternative reading, 'people'. But how striking this plural is, amplifying the first line that God's home is among mortals. There is an apparent universalism to this 'tabernacling' of God among humankind. This dwelling among us echoes both the presence of God in the Old Testament and the incarnation (see Exodus 29:43–45; 2 Chronicles 7:1–3; John 1:14), but the newness here surpasses even these.

Overcoming the difference between heaven and earth has transformative outcomes – death, mourning, crying and pain are no more. All that is negative in human experiences will be removed. While at first sight, the line 'he will wipe away every tear from their eyes' (21:4) might seem to be simply a poetic way of saying the same thing, it takes us further. This is not only because the end of negative experiences is the personal work of God, but even more importantly because the past experiences of death and pain, separation and despair, which result in our tears, will be healed by God's caring presence.

Yet, while all of this is still 'vision' – we live in the light of it but we still journey towards it – holding on to this vision is vital. God's 'new' is not only our destination but the material of the pathway on which we journey.

## Guidelines

Consider whether the call of the disciples or the new beginning described in John 3 more nearly matches your coming-to-faith experience. If neither of these works for you, look for other biblical models. Then give thanks that God in Christ has brought you his new life.

*Here in Revelation (ch. 21—22), Christians are being challenged not to become so absorbed in their needs and tasks that they have no time to look ahead to what God will bring into view.*

REVD JOHN RACKLEY

How can we renew our grasp on the promised future of God?

Which helps you most? Scripture, music, paintings or the 'signposts' we glimpse in the courage, selfless love, generous forgiveness and dedicated service that we come across in others?

Reflect on the 'needs and tasks' that shape your life, making a list of those which demand your attention and energy. Then seek to bring them into the presence of God's new creation.

# Mark 1—3

During 2018 we will read Mark chapters 1—8 in sections of three weeks each, in each of the three editions of *Guidelines*. Our first chunk, starting now, takes us through Mark chapters 1—3. Generally, we will follow the New Revised Standard Version (NRSV), though occasionally I have used my own translation.

What a treat we have in store! Mark's Gospel was probably the first to be written, and so Mark did not know that he was inventing a whole new genre of writing, which we call 'Gospel', as he set out to present Jesus' life and ministry. The little we know about his reasons for writing suggests that Mark wrote it in partnership with Peter, drawing on Peter's memories to produce an 'accurate' account (so second-century Papias tells us), which was not meant to be a chronological record, but a hands-on summary designed to inspire, adapted to the needs of the moment. What precisely those needs were, it is hard to say. Was Mark aiming to support the church facing persecution? Or to resource the church after Peter's death? Or to provide an authorised written record of Jesus' life in the face of a confusion of memories?

Whatever the reasons, we know what we meet when we read: a punchy, vivid, fast-moving narrative, presenting Jesus in a torrent of stories with a sur-prise in every line. Most BRF readers will already be very familiar with Mark. So it is important to try to set aside that familiarity and catch the story again in all its energy and pace. It really seems as though Mark wanted to grab his readers by the shoulders and say, 'Get hold of this – put it down if you dare!'

Some may be familiar with the Mark Drama, which has been presented in many churches in recent years (see **www.themarkdrama.com**). This exploits Mark's fast-paced, bite-sized pattern, and is based on the work of Andrew Page, whose book *The Mark Experiment: How Mark's Gospel can help you know Jesus better* (VTR Publications, 2008) contains fascinating in-sights into the structure of the Gospel. Page thinks that Mark was deliberately designed to be memorable. This book would be my go-to suggestion as a supplement for these notes. If you would like something meatier, my favourite scholarly commentary – readable and full of insight – is Morna Hooker's *The Gospel According to St Mark* (Bloomsbury, 2001).

# 1 The launch

**Mark 1:1–3**

Mark lets us in on the secret underlying his Gospel from the start: 'the beginning of the good news [or 'gospel'] of Jesus Christ, the Son of God' (v. 1). 'Gospels' had not been invented when Mark wrote this, so he is not telling us that this is verse one of his Gospel. Rather, the NRSV is right to translate 'gospel' as 'good news' here. The Greek word *euaggelion* was used in the ancient world of any proclamation designed to be good news for the hearers. And, because he is about to quote Isaiah 40, Mark may be thinking of the prophecy of good news for Zion in Isaiah 40:9.

So it is worth asking: what is the good news contained in the story that begins here? We are used to gospel summaries which say something like: Jesus died for our sins and rose again so that all who believe in him might be forgiven and have eternal life. Is that the shape and content of the good news in Mark? Or does it have different themes and offers? If so, what? We will come back to this as we proceed.

Mark immediately signals a theme important for his presentation of the good news: the fulfilment of scripture. There are few direct Old Testament quotations in Mark, but Old Testament ideas and passages often lie just below the surface – and Mark tells us to be on the lookout for them by these dramatic upfront quotations in verses 2–3. Specifically, they introduce John the Baptist in verse 4 – his is the 'voice of one crying out in the wilderness' (v. 3). But they also look beyond the Baptist and introduce the whole good news; the 'you' addressed in verse 2 ('before your face') is *Israel*. Scripture is being fulfilled in the whole story that follows. The first line of the quotation does not come from Isaiah, but from Exodus 23:20, where it refers to the angel that led Israel through the wilderness to the promised land. This is connected to a line from Malachi 3:1 ('who will prepare your way'), and then to Isaiah 40:3 (v. 3).

Through this collection of verses, Mark appeals also to us, his readers. We too are the 'you' before whom this 'messenger' – John – leads the way, pointing us to Jesus, and calling us to prepare his way into our lives.

# 2 How can we prepare the way?

John the Baptist had a huge impact. Mark doesn't intend us to believe that the entire population of Judah and Jerusalem descended on him all at once (v. 5), but that, over a period of time, *everyone* was touched by his powerful ministry. (The verb phrase 'were baptised' in verse 5 is in the past continuous tense.) He truly did prepare Israel – although, as Mark will show, Israel's leaders remained significantly unready. We see here three key elements in this preparation for the coming of the Lord – for Israel, and for us:

*Into the wilderness.* They leave behind the comforts and securities of home and the city, and seek a place where only rough clothes and 'desert tucker' sustain life (v. 6). The wilderness was the place of true spiritual life, according to Jeremiah (2:2) and Hosea (2:14) – the place where Israel had truly walked with God before.

*Repentance and confession.* In the desert, dispensing with all earthly security and facing God directly, repentance and confession are the only responses possible. John was doing something new and radical, by offering forgiveness just through baptism, not involving sacrifice or the temple in Jerusalem: this will be an issue, as we will see in Mark 2:1–12.

*New expectation and hope.* John points them to a coming one, a great figure who 'will baptise you with the Holy Spirit' (v. 8). Out there in the desert, feeling the presence and hearing the voice of God, it was easier to believe that God was about to do something new and wonderful for Israel – although it's not clear what 'baptism in the Holy Spirit' will look like. Mark has already told us who this 'greater one' will be: the Son of God (v. 1), in whom 'the Lord' himself comes to his people (v. 3).

Later, Jesus will tell his disciples that they must leave everything to follow him – home, family and money. Only so will they be able to 'inherit eternal life' (Mark 10:17, 28–30). That radical commitment and belonging is prefigured here by the streams of people who left their homes and walked into the desert to be baptised by John, realising and confessing their sins, and catching his excitement about the imminent coming of the Lord himself.

These three focuses have inspired Christian spirituality all down the centuries since the crowds streamed out to hear John. Can they inspire your prayer today?

# 3 He arrives

In Mark's fast-paced narrative, the greater one arrives straight away. One of Mark's favourite words is the Greek *euthus*, translated 'immediately' or 'at once'; it occurs no fewer than eleven times in chapter 1 alone, and twice in these verses. When God acts, Mark is saying, there is no delay: *immediately* as Jesus rises from the water, the Spirit descends (v. 10). And *immediately* the Spirit sends Jesus into the desert to be tested (v. 12). This focus on immediacy is in fact the heart of Jesus' message: 'The time has been fulfilled, and the Kingdom of God has drawn near: repent and believe the Gospel!' (v. 15). There are times when the waiting is over, and God calls with urgency, and we simply must respond.

We meet again the three elements of yesterday, refocused now on Jesus:

*Baptism and commitment* (vv. 9–11). Unlike the people, Jesus is not baptised to signal his own repentance and confession. On the contrary, the heavenly voice and the descending Spirit express God's complete satisfaction with his Son: 'with you I am well pleased'. No sins there! And the commitment is not so much Jesus' commitment to God, as God's dedication to him: 'My Son, the Beloved' (v. 11). God's beloved Son stands alongside God's repenting people, one with them.

*Into the wilderness* (vv. 12–13). Jesus is already in the desert for his baptism (v. 4), so we must picture him going further, thrust away by the Spirit to a wildly remote place where he is tested through temptation by Satan. How extraordinary! Matthew and Luke fill out the picture at this point (Matthew 4:1–11; Luke 4:1–13), but Mark leaves us just with the powerful impression that, from Satan's perspective, Jesus must be stopped – and that, from the Spirit's perspective, this battle with Satan is unavoidable.

*New expectation and hope* (vv. 14–15). Now we realise why Satan launches this assault on Jesus. Jesus announces the arrival of God's kingdom, right on time. Standing on the platform, passengers can look along the track and see the train pulling into the station. They need to gather their bags and get ready to board – 'Repent, and believe this good news!' God's 'kingdom' is his powerful 'rule', and the brevity of Mark's summary in verse 15 gives a strong sense of urgency which reaches out and calls all his readers, including us.

# 4  First steps

The powerful arrival of God's kingdom: how will it show itself in the world? What will we see? Mark begins a series of surprising stories to illustrate this, taking us through to the middle of chapter 3. (This first section of his Gospel begins and ends with Jesus calling his disciples by name: see 3:13–19.)

How might we expect God's powerful rule to show itself? Surprisingly, not with a nose-to-nose battle with other claimants to the title 'king' – that will come later. It begins, amazingly, with four fishermen behaving very oddly on the shore of Lake Galilee. Simon and Andrew, and then James and John, abandon their fishing tackle, including (in James and John's case) their father and the whole family business (v. 20), and follow Jesus in response to his strange call, 'Come after me, and I will train you to fish for people!' (v. 17, my translation).

The story is so familiar that its oddness can easily pass us by. All other messianic claimants in the first century (there were several) began by gathering what everyone else perceived as an army intent on overthrowing Roman rule and replacing it (of course) with *God's* rule. Usually these movements began in the desert – as with Jesus here. But Jesus was on his own in the desert, and now recruits his kingdom army to a very different-sounding cause: catching people like fish. Whatever this will mean, the image is not about battle but about *enticement*!

And these four fishermen show what this enticement looks like – being pulled away, just like that, from their nets to follow Jesus, drawn by a powerful summons. Luke and John fill out the picture, and make us aware that this was not the first time the four fishermen had seen or heard Jesus (see especially John 1:40–42). In Luke, this call (Luke 5:10) *follows* Jesus' ministry in Capernaum and a fishing miracle. So there was some background to their immediate and radical response. But for Mark this is kingdom power in action. The word of God's Son has creative power to transform the lives of these four men. And what does it say about the kingdom, that it begins in this simple way? No bellicose posturing in the desert or threats to the powers that be. Just a quiet capturing of followers and a promise that they will capture others in the same way.

# 5 Kingdom authority

**Mark 1:21–28**

'Authority' is the key word here. This little story begins and ends with statements about the astonishment of the synagogue worshippers, in both cases provoked by Jesus' authority – first by the authority of his teaching (v. 22), and then by his authority over the unclean spirit in performing the exorcism (v. 27).

What unites them both is the power of Jesus' *word* – the same power that made the three words, 'Come, follow me', irresistible to Simon, Andrew, James and John (v. 17). The first sets Jesus' authority in contrast to 'the scribes' (v. 22), who typically taught with no authority of their own at all. Their style of teaching is illustrated by the rabbinic teachings surviving from a slightly later period, which consist in discussing and passing on the teaching of revered rabbis of the past, and listing and rehearsing their views. But Jesus teaches 'as one having authority' (v. 22), not needing to defer to the interpretations of others.

Mark frequently tells us that Jesus taught (e.g. 2:13; 4:1; 6:2, 6), but interestingly records much less of his actual teaching than the other Gospel writers. Perhaps that is because of the connection Mark makes in this story between teaching and power: this is 'new teaching with authority' (v. 27), manifested not just in Jesus' words but in his power to heal. This is kingdom authority! Once again it is heading in a unique direction, overthrowing not rival rulers but the power of Satan over people's lives.

It is interesting that the hearers ask no questions about the demon's words, 'I know who you are – the Holy One of God!' It is as though no one actually heard this amazing description. Jesus' command to the demon to 'be silent' (v. 25) – the first of many such commands in Mark – fits with the fact that the synagogue crowd is left with a question about Jesus, not an answer: 'What is this?' (v. 27). Mark surely means this to be a question for his readers, too: what are we dealing with here? Does the kingdom of God truly arrive with Jesus of Nazareth, powerful to deliver the oppressed and to give truth that cuts through the chaos of conflicting opinions and interpretations? Mark's answer is clearly yes, but read on! There are more surprises in store. God's kingdom truly overthrows the kingdoms of this world, because it disrupts them so totally – like Jesus in Capernaum that sabbath day.

# 6 The kingdom brings healing

Jesus' unhesitating healing of Peter's mother-in-law breaches sabbath rules and foreshadows coming conflict (see 3:1–6). All the other Capernaum villagers wait, as they should, until the end of the sabbath at sundown (v. 32), and then descend on Simon and Andrew's house, bringing all their sick and demon-possessed. Jesus heals 'many' of them (v. 34). The difference between 'all' in verse 32 and 'many' in verse 34 might be significant: is Mark implying that Jesus did not heal all the sick who came? Matthew excludes this implication, at the equivalent spot in his Gospel (Matthew 4:23–24; compare 12:15). But later Mark will tell us that Jesus 'could not' heal in Nazareth, where people did not believe in him (Mark 6:5–6). Jesus does not use magical power that bypasses its human setting: his healings are part of the preaching of the kingdom, and the response of faith to that message is vital.

So why does Jesus seek to conceal his identity here (v. 34)? Is it not the essential heart of the good news that kingdom power is operating because the king, the Son of God, has come? The German Bible scholar Wilhelm Wrede famously suggested that this 'messianic secret' (as he called it) was an invention by Mark to explain why the early church believed Jesus was the Messiah when, in fact, Jesus never claimed that. The fact is, Jesus *did* claim it, but in secret. Wrede simply shifts the puzzle, however – leaving us wondering how the church came to believe that Jesus was the Messiah at all. It is better to wonder why Jesus announced the arrival of the kingdom but wanted his own identity kept quiet, both by demons and by those he healed (see 1:44; 3:12; 5:43; 7:36; 8:30).

This difficult question obviously connects with Jesus' use of parables (see 4:11–12) and also with his strange name for himself, 'Son of Man' (see e.g. 2:10, 28) – so we will come back to it in future passages. But an answer that suggests itself here concerns precisely that response of faith so vital for the healings: faith must not be compelled by loud public proclamations, but must grow quietly, hidden in people's hearts. See Matthew's explanation of the 'messianic secret' in Matthew 12:16–21, quoting Isaiah 42:2–3, 'no one will hear his voice in the streets. A bruised reed he will not break.' Jesus' quiet gentleness requires secrecy.

# Guidelines

There is much to prompt thought and prayer this week. We can focus it around the following question: where and how do we see the kingdom of God arriving in the world today? Our thoughts on this will expand as we dig deeper into Mark, but already he has prompted some fascinating reflections.

*The kingdom and Jesus.* For Mark, they go together. The kingdom of God cannot arrive without Jesus – and where he is, there the kingdom is. But he does not have to be recognised for kingdom power to work through him: in fact, he seems to prefer it when he is *not* recognised. Why would this be?

*The kingdom and healing.* Where the kingdom is, there human needs are met and well-being is enhanced. Faith is the key to this power – would Simon's mother-in-law have been healed if the first disciples had not thought to tell Jesus about her (v. 30)? Probably not.

*The kingdom and the powers of evil.* 'Unclean spirits' (v. 23) are abroad in the world today – wherever people are trapped by greed, fear, war, injustice, racial hatred and sexual fantasy. We need the power of the kingdom to deliver us.

*The kingdom and the call to follow.* Immediately Mark presents us with the inner appeal that Jesus issues: the four fishermen respond in that dramatic way because their hearts have been captured by Jesus. Even though they are still deeply puzzled by him (as we will see), they want to know him better and are ready to sacrifice 'everything' (Mark 10:28) in order to achieve that.

All four of these truths about the kingdom can be manifested and expressed in and through the church of Jesus Christ – but only the last *must* be. The church is the gathering of those who share a call to follow Jesus Christ. The power of the kingdom, manifested in the overthrow of evil and in the blessing of human life, does not even have to be explicitly linked to the name of Jesus, let alone to his church. But Jesus is that Lord, the Son of God, in whom alone God's rule of healing and freedom from evil is established in the earth, even if he keeps himself incognito!

Allow these kingdom truths to shape your reflection and prayer in response to Mark today.

# 1 Prayer and mission

Book titles and their authors' names sometimes have unfortunate overtones. Browsing once in a second-hand bookshop in Salisbury, I was electrified to discover *In the Secret Place of the Most High* by the aptly named A.J. Gossip. Gossip was actually a distinguished Scottish preacher and theologian, who would have hated the idea that prayer (or preaching) was about digging out heavenly secrets and passing them on with a nudge and a wink. For him, prayer was much more as we see it in today's passage, the essential power-house of kingdom calling and work. Even for Jesus, to be *publicly engaged* with people (v. 39) meant being *privately resourced* with his Father (v. 35).

Jesus' relationship with his Father clearly comes first – before the needs of the Capernaum residents who come chasing to find him, having heard about the healings of the previous evening. And even when Simon and the others find him, Jesus' reaction is not to rush back into Capernaum to meet the needs of 'everyone' (p. 37) who is looking for him. He keeps the wider vision clear: 'Let us go on to the neighbouring villages, so that I may preach there too. That's why I came out!' (v. 38). 'Came out' clearly relates to 'went out' in verse 35; in other words, Jesus left Capernaum before dawn with the intention not of going back there, but of going on to other villages to 'preach there too'.

Jesus' 'preaching' in Capernaum was two-pronged: first he *proclaimed* the kingdom in the synagogue, then he *demonstrated* the kingdom in the street outside Simon's house. He then does the same elsewhere, as Mark summarises it: 'he went throughout Galilee, proclaiming the message in their synagogues and casting out demons' (v. 39). This is the 'teaching with authority' we met in verse 27 – teaching whose truth is shown by the power of its application in practice. The kingdom truly has 'come near' with such teaching (v. 15)!

There is so much to reflect on here for mission today – mission which is rooted in prayer, in a living relationship with God, which springs straight from that relationship, rather than simply as a response to to the immediate pressure of human need; and mission in which *word* and *deed* match each other as coordinated testimony to the kingdom. That's what we need!

## 2 Power, purity and preaching

This is such a beautiful story – undoubtedly chosen by Mark because it holds so many themes (and surprises) vital for his presentation of Jesus. The place to begin is at Mark's extraordinary use of the word 'preach' in verse 45 (NRSV 'proclaim'), backed up – in case we should miss it – by the explanation 'spread the word'. These expressions mean much more than that the leper goes around telling people about his healing. He has become a kingdom preacher, like Jesus himself (see 1:38–39; 2:2) – albeit against Jesus' instructions (vv. 43–44). Though he should not be speaking, except non-verbally to the priest, there is something about this man's 'testimony' (v. 44) which holds the whole good news, the 'word' which Jesus himself preaches. What could this be?

The answer is to do with his particular disease. Unlike the fever Simon's mother-in-law had (v. 30), this man's leprosy makes him 'unclean', which means that he is permanently outside the reaches of the religion of the day, unable to participate in worship or festivals – and unable to live normally, for anyone or anything he touched would immediately become 'unclean', and special ceremonies would then be required to restore purity. (See Leviticus 13—14 for the details.) 'Unclean' is completely different from 'infectious'.

Here's the vital point: when Jesus touches the man, Jesus should be made ritually 'unclean' in this sense. But the leper already has the conviction that Jesus can 'cleanse' him (v. 40) – and sure enough, when Jesus touches him the movement goes the other way: instead of his 'uncleanness' expelling Jesus' purity, Jesus' powerful touch drives purity back into the leper's body. How glorious is that? This gift of purity restores the man to fellowship both with God and with his family and people. This is indeed the good news – as we shall see further tomorrow.

What motivates Jesus? 'Moved with pity' may not be the right translation in verse 41. As the NRSV notes, some ancient manuscripts of Mark have 'moved with anger', and personally I think this is more likely to be what Mark originally wrote. Something in Jesus boils over at the sight of this man, cut off from God and family by this terrible state of impurity. The kingdom welcomes all such, driving uncleanness back, bringing them in from the cold. Jesus gladly steps out of line to make it happen.

# 3 Friends, faith and forgiveness

Here is another dramatic story – again with vital themes for our understanding of Jesus. We will take two days to think about it!

The faith of the four friends is one of those key themes. 'When Jesus saw their faith' (v. 5) is the turning point of the story. Without that, nothing would have happened. But like Jesus' own faith in 1:41, which moved him to reach out and touch the leper, so the friends' faith is active and bold. Up on to the roof they go, because they are so desperate to get their friend to Jesus. This is what Paul calls 'faith working through love' (Galatians 5:6). Interestingly, the friends must have felt sure that the homeowner would forgive them for ruining the roof – which anticipates Jesus' words to the paralytic as he lands on the floor in front of him: 'Son, your sins are forgiven!' (v. 5).

But the muttering scribes know that Jesus is talking about much more than the sin of criminal damage to a roof. The background to his words, and to their question in verse 7, is the conviction, universally held at this time, that physical disability and illness were a punishment for sin. Later rabbis even tied specific illnesses to specific sins. It went without saying that this man was a sinner; this was shown by his physical state. The paralytic himself undoubtedly believed this, too.

This is why the physical healing can work as a proof that Jesus has 'authority on earth to forgive sins' (v. 10): if God is willing to give the man health by Jesus' word, then his sins must be forgiven, too. Jesus elsewhere disputes this automatic connection between sin and sickness (see John 9:1–3), but here he works with it because it is the universal assumption of everyone in (or on!) that house that day.

Jesus' word of command to the paralytic is crystal clear: 'Rise, pick up your mat, and go home!' (v. 11). But notably he does *not* tell him to go and offer a sacrifice or a thank offering in the temple in Jerusalem – the normal route to forgiveness. No further steps are needed. Forgiveness has been given, and restoration is complete. This bypassing of the 'cult' – that is, the religion of the day so valued by the muttering scribes of verse 6 – is another key theme here. We will come back to this.

# 4 Who is this?

Who is this Jesus? At first the scribes call Jesus' words 'blasphemy' – no mere mortal can speak this way, proclaiming God's forgiveness (v. 7). But at the end, maybe at least some of them are part of the 'all' who are amazed and glorify God for what they have seen (v. 12). Who is he?

We might conclude that Jesus shows his deity here – after all, aren't the scribes correct, that only God can forgive sins? So isn't Jesus acting as God here, both in the forgiveness and in the healing? But that is not Jesus' own claim. Instead, he refers to himself obliquely as 'the Son of Man': 'so that you may know that the Son of Man has authority on earth to forgive sins' (v. 10). This is the first of 14 places in Mark where Jesus uses this strange expression of himself. It never appears outside the Gospels or on anyone else's lips in referring to him, except in Revelation 1:13 and 14:14. It's not an obvious claim to deity. Is this another instance of the 'secrecy motif' – Jesus veiling his true identity? But what might he be hiding?

Perhaps the truth is that Jesus – and Mark, presenting him – wants to make us think. The scribes call his words blasphemy, but prophets could pronounce God's forgiveness on his behalf, and regularly did. John the Baptist does it (Mark 1:4). And ironically Jesus immediately shows prophetic awareness of the scribes' hidden mutterings (v. 8). Will they at least be ready to see him as a prophet?

'Son of Man', however, might prod them to see more than just a prophet. There is some evidence that in Aramaic it could be just a slightly odd mode of self-reference, rather like the old-fashioned 'one' sometimes associated with Her Majesty. So they could have thought it was just Jesus' quirky way of speaking. But on the other hand, maybe lying in the background is the mysterious and powerful vision in Daniel 7, in which 'one like a son of man' appears before God in heaven and is invested with God's authority – in fact with 'dominion, glory and kingship' to rule on his behalf and to receive the worship of the nations (Daniel 7:13–14). But it would be a huge step of faith to see Jesus in that light – wouldn't it? Faith like that of the four friends?

# 5 Jesus – down and out

Issues of sin and of purity went hand in hand at this time. In the story of the leper (1:40–45) we saw Jesus driving back impurity and making the leper 'clean'. In the story of the paralytic it was sin's turn to be banished by Jesus' powerful healing authority. Now the two issues come together – literally, as the impure and the sinful unite around Levi's dinner table to eat with Levi's chief guest and new master, Jesus. 'Why does he eat with tax collectors and sinners?' say the 'scribes of the Pharisees' (v. 16), peering in through the door and holding their noses.

Actually, we mustn't mock the Pharisees for their passionate concern for purity. It led them to develop an incredibly disciplined lifestyle of detailed obedience to the demands of the law. But it led them also to a fear of contamination through contact with impurity – especially through contact with Gentiles (this is why tax collectors were numbered among the impure) and with all other 'sinners' whose lifestyle did not match Pharisaic purity standards. This lies behind their question in verse 16 – Jesus is in danger! He will contract uncleanness, just from the contact. But we already know from the story of the leper that there is no danger to Jesus. The opposite happens: impurity is driven back.

It is amazing – and wonderful – to see in the Gospels how sinners felt attracted to Jesus. Like the four fishermen, Levi springs to his feet to follow Jesus (v. 14), and 'many' others do the same (v. 15). Normally shame shuts us away from human contact, especially from any who might see us as we really are and expose our shamefulness. But in Jesus' case, sinners *knew* that he *knew* them, and that he wanted to be with them nonetheless – indeed that he celebrated his contact with them. So they were drawn to him. It seems that forgiveness, like purity, just oozed out of him and spread all around, 'infecting' all who wanted to be with him. Then the party started! One writer, commenting on Jesus' use of table fellowship, says that it must have looked like there was a perpetual party going on round him.

Jesus' words in verse 17 spring across the centuries and invite us all to let him see our shame and our sin – however painful – and to let him into those secret places where we store our deepest feelings of regret, remorse or self-loathing.

# 6 New wine

Mark continues his sequence of stories dealing with Jesus' impact on current religious practices and ideas. Fasting – a sign of repentance, grief, religious intensity and deep spiritual seriousness – was required by the law once a year, on the Day of Atonement (Leviticus 23:29), but the Pharisees practised it twice a week (Luke 18:12), in fact on Mondays and Thursdays, the second and fifth days. The disciples of John clearly did the same. In Matthew's version of this story, they themselves approach Jesus with their puzzled question, 'Why do we and the Pharisees fast often, but your disciples do not fast?' (Matthew 9:14). Is Jesus not serious about spiritual discipline?

For Jesus, spiritual life is not about what you do, but about who you know. His beautiful parable in verses 19–20 implicitly casts himself in the role of the bridegroom: while the celebration is going on, none of the groom's party will want to fast. Jesus' own presence makes fasting inappropriate.

What an extraordinary reply! It means that Jesus himself does not need to use fasting in order to relate deeply to his Father, and so his followers don't need to either, while he is with them. They might need to later – but only when the loss of their relational connection with him plunges them into grief (v. 20).

The pair of little parables in verses 21–22 then unpack this extraordinary newness. A whole new relationship with God is now on offer, summarised by Jesus' great announcement 'the Kingdom of God has come near!' (1:15). This new relationship can't be contained in the old packaging – it simply shatters it. A party is more fitting than a fast.

The New Wine movement, which started with its first summer festival at Shepton Mallet in 1989, has now expanded into a countrywide network with a range of events all aiming to let the Spirit of Christ renew his church in tradition-busting ways. We can still become wedded to traditions that cannot contain him – especially if (as was the case with the Pharisees) the traditions still hold real spiritual power to touch and bless us. But they may not be sufficient for him, even if they are sufficient for us! This is why a *relational* spirituality always needs to move us beyond a traditional one. We need to party with the bridegroom!

# Guidelines

There is a multitude of themes to draw out of this week's readings. We started with prayer (1:35) – in fact Mark probably wants us to see this whole sequence of events as arising from, and energised by, Jesus' prayerful relationship with his Father. That's what it's all about: the new relationship with God which this arrival of his kingdom announces and illustrates, shown first by Jesus himself as he breaks old boundaries, touches the leper, proclaims forgiveness and welcomes the impure into party relationship with himself.

What has touched you most within this sequence of stories? It would be good to stay with that as you reflect, and to turn it into prayer. Each of us will carry something different away, partly because we are all different, but partly also because there is such richness in these stories.

For me the story of the four friends stands out as I reflect now (2:3): their vibrant, bold, boundary-breaking (literally!) confidence that Jesus can heal the one they love; the way Jesus responds to *their* faith as he gives forgiveness to their paralysed friend (2:5); and the way in which this seems to foreshadow the new community of the impure and the sinful, gathered around Jesus, whose authority pronounces us forgiven and welcome at the feast (2:15). Is that not a wonderful picture of his church?

The only entry requirement for that feast is the willingness to acknowledge ourselves impure and sinful. If we are not in that place, we must stay outside. As Jesus says, the healthy need no doctor, only the sick (2:17). The willingness to allow ourselves to be sick – to be sinful, shamed, weak and unclean – is the essential entrance ticket to that feast. Nothing else can get us in – no status or giftedness, no intellectual powers or spiritual insights, no achievement or reputation. All this must be checked in at the door. If we have none of that to start with, so much the better for us – there is less to lose!

This is the paradox of the kingdom of God. In different ways, we all hold on to the right to reign in our own lives. God calls us to lay that down in order to be blessed by his reign. What might this mean for you?

# 1 The final word

**Mark 2:23–28**

The interpretation of scripture has been a hidden theme in the stories we've met so far, because the Pharisees and other passionate adherents of the religion of purity thought that they were simply upholding and obeying the clear teaching of scripture. Now that theme bubbles up to the surface, around the specific issue of sabbath observance – the fourth commandment (Exodus 20:8–11). What will be Jesus' attitude to scripture and its interpretation?

The disciples are exercising a permission specifically granted by the law, as they wander through the field plucking ears of corn, rubbing them in their hands to remove the husks and then eating the grain (see Deuteronomy 23:25). But the Pharisees see their action as *threshing*, which was included in the list of 39 activities called 'work' and thus forbidden on the sabbath. So 'not lawful' (v. 24) means 'contrary to traditional interpretation and application of the law'.

Jesus' reply has two parts to it, both touching on the interpretation of scripture. The first, in verses 25–26, concerns a particular story and is a kind of 'softener' leading into his second and main point, in verses 27–28. The story of David and the 'shewbread' in 1 Samuel 21:1–6 concerns a time when, on the run from Saul, David persuaded the priest to give him the special 'holy' bread which was kept in the sanctuary, and which – *according to tradition* – only the priests were supposed to eat. Jesus is pointing to a scriptural instance where, for good reasons, the usual interpretative application of the principles of holiness was set aside. He's saying scripture shows that our interpretations should sometimes be set aside.

Then comes the punchline in verses 27–28, which itself has two parts. Firstly, *an interpretational principle* (v. 27): look underneath, and ask what the purpose is. In this case, it's about meeting human need. Jesus gives priority to the sabbath command to 'rest', rather than the command 'do no work'. And secondly, *an authority principle*: as the Son of Man, *he* has the authority to define how this command should be interpreted and applied. They need to listen to him. This is powerful and dramatic. Once again, his meaning is veiled behind the enigmatic use of 'Son of Man'. But any Pharisees who caught the allusion to Daniel 7:13 would know what Jesus is claiming here.

# 2 Life – and death

Jesus is in the synagogue again, but this time the Pharisees are watching in case he performs another healing, 'so that they might accuse him' (v. 2) – that is, bring him into court on a formal charge of sabbath-breaking, which carries the death penalty (see Exodus 31:14). Healing, you see, is *work*. This is a rule affecting chiefly doctors, who were allowed to perform emergency treatments on the sabbath, but not to treat long-term, chronic conditions like a withered hand. Interestingly, no one doubts that Jesus can heal miraculously. It's just about *when* he does it!

Jesus addresses this distinction between acute and chronic conditions elsewhere (Matthew 12:11; Luke 13:14). Here he appeals to a fundamental principle in the law: 'Is it lawful on the sabbath to do good or to do harm, to save life or to kill?' (v. 4). There is huge irony here, in that he then does good and gives life to the man with the withered hand, but the Pharisees leave the synagogue and 'immediately' – that is, on that very sabbath – start plotting to kill Jesus (v. 6). Their action is their answer to his question.

The Pharisees think they are upholding scripture by seeking the prescribed death penalty for someone who wilfully violates sabbath rules, and they manage to persuade the Herodians to join them. Normally these groups were poles apart – but the Herodians have political clout, and might be able actually to carry out an execution. Jesus, on the other hand, claims that *he* is upholding sabbath law by doing good and giving life, because that is the purpose of the commandment: to enhance and sustain life by requiring rest from labour. It is modelled on God's rest after creation (Exodus 20:11), and reflects his deliverance of his people from slavery (Deuteronomy 5:15). We are in his image, and therefore we rest, and seek to bring rest to others. And we are no longer slaves, and therefore we rest, and seek to bring freedom from bondage to others. In Luke 13:16 Jesus makes explicit this link between the sabbath and freedom from bondage.

Each view angers the exponents of the other (vv. 5–6). And so much is at stake – both the man's freedom from disability, and ultimately Jesus' own life. The Pharisees' view will prevail, and Jesus will be killed – but thereby he will establish his reading of scripture, and 'give life' to the world.

# 3 Flocking to Jesus

Mark completes the first section of his Gospel with two paragraphs (today's and tomorrow's) summarising the story so far. Today we see 'a great multitude… in great numbers' (vv. 7–8) flocking to Jesus from a huge area – much bigger than the area touched by John the Baptist (1:5) – all seeking healing. Tomorrow we will see Jesus' response to this vast tide of human need: expanding his initial group of five (1:16–20; 2:13), he will appoint seven more to extend his reach.

Jesus' response to his awful reception in the synagogue and the threat to his life (vv. 5–6) is to leave town and head for the lake, where much bigger crowds can get close to him (see 1:45). But he is in danger of being crushed (v. 9), because the word has got around that all people need to do is to touch him (v. 10). Mark describes a really alarming situation, with Jesus being pressed down to the water's edge by a crowd so eager to get to him that he has to retreat into a boat for his own safety. In verse 10 Mark describes the people's diseases as (literally) 'scourges', reflecting their belief that the illnesses were punishments for sin. So Jesus' healing power – as in 2:10–11 – is a wonderful expression of a God who is willing to forgive and welcome sinners in their desperate need.

Prominent in the crowd are people afflicted by demons, and once again Jesus tries to shut them up when they cry out his identity (v. 11). Mark has done his own crying out, of course, in his introduction (1:1). Would Jesus approve of that upfront announcement, or would he tell Mark to cool it, too? The voice from heaven breaks the same prohibition in 1:11. The point is – as we will see in chapter 8 – faith can never be compelled, and must always rest on people's own conviction arising from *their own* encounter with Jesus. It can't be second-hand, and certainly can't be based on testimony from demons. Mark has flagged his conviction at the start, but he gives plenty of reasons within the story for *disbelieving* that – indeed for executing Jesus as a blasphemer and lawbreaker, if we should feel inclined to do that. With whom will we, Mark's readers, agree?

The question of who exactly this Jesus is becomes one of the main themes in the next section of the Gospel (3:20–6:6).

# 4 Chosen, called and named

Scriptural allusions can be so subtle. At first sight, verse 13 reads simply as stage directions ahead of the appointment of the twelve which follows – 'he went up the mountain and called to him those whom he wanted, and they came to him'. But mountains are potent symbols in the Bible. See Hebrews 12:18–24 for a passage drawing on the rich and powerful imagery associated with the two greatest biblical mountains, Sinai and Zion. Here we can't help but be reminded of Exodus 19, where Moses goes up Mount Sinai to meet with the Lord himself and to receive the law for Israel (Exodus 19:3). But the parallel is not actually between Jesus and Moses, for in Exodus the Lord calls Moses to the top of the mountain, where the Lord commissions him to speak to the people on his behalf (Exodus 19:20). So here in Mark the *chosen twelve* stand in Moses' shoes, and Jesus represents God himself, appointing 'those he wanted' (v. 13) to speak and act on his behalf (vv. 14–15). The mountain symbolism gives us a whole new perspective on this appointment. This truly is the kingdom *of God* arriving for Israel.

The role of apostle is beautifully defined in verses 14–15 – just like Moses in Exodus, in fact: 'he appointed twelve, whom he also named apostles, to be with him, and to be sent out to preach and to have authority to cast out demons'. Moses spends much time with the Lord in Exodus, and then comes to the people bearing the authority of the Lord himself. So also here, though now healing is added to the authority to speak God's word.

The naming that follows reinforces this sense of the Lord's authority, for Jesus not only *chooses* the twelve from the wider circle of disciples, but also *renames* several of them. In the mixed Hebrew-Greek culture of this time people often had both a Hebrew and a Greek name, and here Jesus gives Simon a new Greek name (v. 16: Peter – the Rock). The renaming of James and John (v. 17) is more than just a jokey nickname reflecting their passionate nature – he gives them a shared name that allows them truly to own who they are. That's vital for apostles, both then and now: only those who have been led to know *themselves* deeply, as well as the Lord, can truly represent him.

# 5 The power of God?

The next section of Mark begins here, taking us through to 6:6 – a section which revolves around the question, 'Who is this Jesus? Is he really the Son of God as Mark claims (1:1)?'

We first meet the crowd, who are so enthusiastic about Jesus that he has no time to eat (v. 20). But then there is a dash of icy cold water – Jesus' own family think he has gone mad and set out to get him (v. 21; the NRSV speculatively but wrongly uses the word 'people' here, to let his family off the hook). We will find out tomorrow what happens when they arrive (vv. 31–35).

Next we meet the 'scribes who came down from Jerusalem' (v. 22). This description implies that they are an official investigative panel, appointed to reach an official verdict about this strange preacher who casts out demons and heals, but breaks the sabbath law. Their decision is that Jesus is possessed by Beelzebub and employs demonic power to cast out demons. (Beelzebub is a roundabout name for the devil, thus avoiding direct reference. It is not only in J.K. Rowling's Potterverse that the arch-enemy is 'He Who Must Not Be Named'!)

Jesus responds to this terrible verdict graciously and patiently (vv. 23–27): why would Satan employ his own power against himself? This would be suicidal for the powers of evil. No – Jesus must be exercising a power greater than that of the 'strong man' (v. 27), and by using this imagery Jesus alludes gently to Isaiah 49:24–25, where God himself promises to rescue Israel from the clutches of 'the mighty' and 'the tyrant'.

Then he adds a solemn warning (vv. 28–30), resting on the counterclaim that the Holy Spirit empowers his kingdom preaching and healing (1:10). It is important to see that Jesus does not accuse the scribes of having committed the sin of blasphemy against the Holy Spirit, so that they are now unforgiveably guilty. He is not reaching a verdict here, unlike them. The phrase 'guilty of an eternal sin' (v. 29) would be better translated 'liable to an eternal sin' – that is, this *may* be how they land up. (The same word is used in Matthew 5:22, where similarly Jesus' point is warning, not condemnation.) If they *persist* in saying this about him, then finally their sin will be an unforgiveable blasphemy, so serious is it. The stakes could not be higher!

# 6 Family, old and new

Mark 3:31–35

Mark loves wrapping one story round another – we will meet this technique several times. He begins the story about Jesus' family in v. 21, dropping the bombshell that they do not support his ministry (compare John 7:5). In fact, they think he has gone mad. But then Mark breaks off and tells the story about the delegation of scribes. This heightens the suspense surrounding the visit of Jesus' family, for madness was widely ascribed to satanic activity. So will his family agree that he is possessed by Beelzebub – even if they want to take him away and look after him, rather than execute him as a blasphemer?

They arrive and stand outside, expecting Jesus to respect them, excuse himself from the crowd in the house and come to meet them (v. 31). Jesus may do this eventually (Mark does not say), but first he responds with extraordinary, offensive words that surely confirm their view that he has gone mad: 'looking around at those sitting in a circle about him, he said, "Look – my mother and my brothers! Whoever does the will of God – that person is my brother, and sister, and mother!"' (vv. 34–35).

In Jewish culture at this time, family was extremely important, because it gave people a sense of place within God's people. People could recite their family tree, and knew which of the twelve tribes they belonged to. Some were even still living on the plot of land originally given to their family under Joshua (Joshua 18—22), although most had lost that precise connection by the first century AD. So for Jesus to question his connection with his family in this way is staggering, and deeply offensive to his waiting brothers and mother. But at the same time, the very radicalness of this tells us something vital about the kingdom of God: it really is new wine that breaks the old wineskins, because it creates a whole new family structure and way of belonging. Family is now the circle of those who sit around Jesus to learn from him, and who thus 'do the will of God'. Doing God's will no longer means belonging obediently to 'old' Israel, enjoying the family location he has given, but hearing a new word from his Son, and sharing a new life with him. Radical indeed. We will see more of this when we return to Mark later this year.

# Guidelines

Again, it is vital to let the Lord impress his word upon you, personally. What stands out for you especially in this week's readings? Look back over Mark 2:23—3:35 and allow a particular verse, word or theme to stand out for you. Then spend some time quietly allowing the Holy Spirit to develop that thought for you, leading your reflections on it. There are so many themes here which might be vital for you.

To kick-start your reflections, here are the verses which seem to be the key ones in this section. What do they say to you, as you hold your life openly before the Lord?

- 'The sabbath was made for us, not we for the sabbath' (2:27).
- 'The Son of Man is Lord of the sabbath' (2:28).
- 'He looked round at them with anger, grieved at their hardness of heart' (3:5).
- 'He looked round at those sitting in a circle about him and said, "Here are my mother and my brothers!"' (3:35).
- 'The unclean spirits, when they saw him, fell before him and cried out, saying, "You are the Son of God!"' (3:11).
- 'He went up the mountain and called those he wanted to him, and they went to him' (3:13).

Underlying all these stories is the powerful call of the Son of God. He draws huge crowds to him, and those whom he wants are willing to leave their current lives and follow him, even though he says such difficult and challenging things. He stands out boldly, proclaiming a new word from God that divides the people who hear it. Some can't stand the newness and reject it, while to others it's fascinating and compelling, and they are willing 'to be with him, and to be sent out to preach and to have authority to cast out demons' (3:14–15).

Where are you with the call of the Son of God on your life?

---

**FURTHER READING**

James R. Edwards, *The Gospel According to Mark* (Eerdmans/Apollos, 2002).

Morna Hooker, *The Gospel According to St Mark* (Continuum, 1991).

Andrew Page, *The Mark Experiment: How Mark's Gospel can help you know Jesus better* (VTR Publications, 2005).

Tom Wright, *Mark for Everyone* (SPCK, 2001).

# Work

> We may love our work, hate our work, find meaning in our work or none, but it's what we do all day long, and it shapes us.

So writes Joanna Biggs in *All Day Long: A portrait of Britain at work* (Serpent's Tail, 2015). It's an enjoyably absorbing read, offering glimpses into the lives of 30 or so different people – such as a pot-glazing supervisor from Stoke-on-Trent, a fishmonger from Belfast and a care worker from Newcastle, along with shoemakers, baristas, a stay-at-home mum, a goldsmith's apprentice, a rabbi and so on.

There are struggles – the baristas lose their bonus if they don't display 'passion'; the cleaner has to fight for a living wage; the legal-aid lawyer had to wrestle with budget cuts. Yet what also emerges is how hard people work, even though they have seemingly little to show for it; how much satisfaction people get from working; and how (in many cases) such satisfaction is not dependent on the salary earned.

All this resonates with a Christian perspective flowing out of scripture. As we will see in our readings over the next two weeks, work is one of the ways we are made to function as those created in the image of the God who designed work to be fulfilling not frustrating. But work – like all things – was impacted by human rebellion against God and alienation from each other. Our daily labour brings with it a daily reminder that the world remains out of kilter with God's design, with the twin distortions of idolatry and idleness, the blight of modern-day slavery alongside unemployment, and bosses and workforces treating one another with inherent suspicion.

Yet there is hope, for work is not just a way to pass time and make money, but a service we render to Christ himself (Colossians 3:23). Work is a crucible for discipleship, a means to grow as a follower of Jesus, even in mundane tasks, such as writing an email, placing an order, servicing a boiler, tightening a bolt or changing a nappy. Seeing work – paid or unpaid – as an arena to serve Christ won't necessarily deal with all our frustrations, but it will put them in proper perspective as we take our place as God's stewards in his ongoing governance of the world.

Quotations are from the New International Version (Anglicised).

# 1 God at work

**Genesis 1:1—2:3**

The first step in our journey of understanding work starts not with ourselves, but with God – as a worker. From the beginning of the biblical story, on the very first page, we see that work is bound up with who God is and what God does. Several times in Genesis 1 we are told God 'creates', and that he 'does' certain acts. In Genesis 2:2–3, God's activity during the week of creation is specifically referred to as 'work'.

So it is that Genesis 1 shows God himself working – commanding, building, forming, doing quality control – and then resting too. God takes what is 'formless and empty' (1:2) and 'works' to form it (separating light from darkness, water from sky, land from sea) and then to fill it (with vegetation; the sun, moon and stars; fish, birds and animals; and human beings). Unlike how gods were portrayed in other cultures in the ancient Near East, the biblical God is not some cosmic, aloof deity who doesn't get his hands dirty. Not only is work not beneath God, but he takes delight in it, as he stands back and – like a satisfied labourer at the end of the day – declares all his work to be good (1:31). From beginning to end, this portrayal of God dignifies everyday labour.

Of course, God's work doesn't stop after the opening chapters of Genesis. In *God the Worker*, Robert J. Banks explores a number of images used throughout the Bible to describe God, such as shepherd, potter, craft worker, builder, architect, weaver, gardener, farmer, musician and artist – images drawn not simply from human life in general but from the realm of human work in particular.

All this encourages us to think about how our work reflects dimensions of God's own work. In what ways does our work provide a context in which others can thrive? In what ways does our work bring order out of chaos? In what ways does our work demonstrate creativity, provide for others or produce joy?

Already, then, we get a strong hint that work is not some necessary evil that came into the world at a later point. That is reinforced with the creation of men and women, to which we turn next.

# 2 Created to work

Genesis 1:26—2:15

Cultures surrounding Israel told stories of people being made as slaves of the gods, to do the labour the gods didn't want to do, with work portrayed as a burden. Genesis, however, gives men and women a status and responsibility not found in other worldviews. Work is seen not as a chore or as a curse, but as an essential part of our God-given dignity and identity.

God creates men and women in his image to exercise dominion on his behalf over creation (1:26–28). As the account continues, we get an indication of how that dominion will express itself. There was 'no one to work the ground' (2:5), and so 'the Lord took the man and put him in the Garden of Eden to work it and take care of it' (2:15). The two verbs in the NIV translation of Genesis 2:15 as 'work' and 'take care' are both found elsewhere in the Old Testament in contexts of worship – where work and service and worship are linked together. They are used (for instance) of the role of the priests and Levites in offering daily sacrifices to God in the work of the tabernacle, guarding the holiness of God's sanctuary.

In the first place, the language about being fruitful, filling the earth and subduing it (1:26–28) refers to the building of families, the growing of crops, the breeding of animals and the tending of the garden to which Adam and Eve are called. Creation requires cultivation. But such cultivation includes by extension the development of culture and civilisation. It's an important reminder on the opening pages of the Bible that work isn't restricted to the jobs we get paid for, but encompasses the whole range of activities which build society and which steward the resources of creation in the cause of human flourishing.

God designed men and women to contribute to the nurturing and cultivation of his creation, and to reflect something of his own rule in doing so. Properly understood, then, our work is an act of worship, which might reframe how we think about it, helping us to see what we do in our everyday life as an integral part of our honouring of God and our service to others.

# 3 Frustrated with work

For many of us, work can be a drag. Not all the time, to be sure, but there are enough periods of frustration to make us dream of escaping to a simpler life without jammed photocopiers, rude customers, demanding managers and unrealistic deadlines. If God devised work, shouldn't we expect it to be fulfilling? As we have seen in our readings so far, we are created in the image of a God who finds satisfaction and delight in work, and who designed work to be fulfilling not frustrating, pleasurable not painful. But work – like all things – was impacted by human rebellion against God and our falling out with each other.

Work itself is not cursed, but nor does it escape the distorting and disintegrating effects of sin, such that it has become 'painful toil' (Genesis 3:17). We're able to enjoy the fruit of our labours, but only by the 'sweat of [our] brow' and by contending with 'thorns and thistles' along the way (Genesis 3:18–19).

Ecclesiastes provides a voice for the frustrations we might feel. Work can appear to be 'meaningless' (1:3; 2:11). In 2:17–23, the writer reflects on the temporary and fleeting nature of what's accomplished through labour when death eventually intervenes, and the pressures of work that occupy our waking and sleeping thoughts, and he despairs at the apparent futility of it all.

Even so, the writer can also confess that 'there is nothing better for people than to be happy and to do good while they live… and find satisfaction in all their toil – this is the gift of God' (3:12–13). As a gift, work can be enjoyed (3:22) as something that brings satisfaction (5:18–19), and even pleasure (8:15). The key, in 2:24–26, seems to be not seeking delight in what we gain from work, but seeing good in the work itself, as from the hand of God.

Workplaces can be painful and messy, with strained relationships, where the work itself is difficult. Yet we have sufficient examples in scripture – Joseph, Ruth, Daniel and Esther – to show that God works through us in difficult situations, often in spite of our flaws. Beyond this, the good news is that the fall of humankind into sin is not the last chapter in the biblical story. There is good news for work.

# 4 Renewal of work

Psalm 8, part of which is cited in this passage, echoes the language and ideas of Genesis 1. But its apparent upshot – that men and women are crowned with glory and honour, and given dominion over creation – simply doesn't match our experience. Though formed in the image of God, our representation of his rule – not least in the sphere of work – is distorted. Plus, death so clearly thwarts human dominion in the world, and no one has found a way through that barrier.

Except, as the writer to the Hebrews tells us, there is one human being who has fulfilled the destiny for which we were made. Jesus, himself made lower than the angels, because of his suffering and death on behalf of others, has now been crowned with glory and honour and reigns over all things, breaking even the power of the devil and death itself (vv. 14–15). We don't yet see God's final plan for humanity and creation completed, 'but we do see Jesus' (v. 9). The rule described in Psalm 8, which so easily eludes us, has become a reality in him.

It is sometimes suggested that Jesus has completed the command to rule given to Adam and Eve, and so it no longer applies to us today. But, if anything, his dominion over all things makes the original creation mandate even more significant. As Christians, we are being remade in the image of Christ, restored under Christ's lordship to what was lost through Adam and Eve, so as to bring glory to God in all we do.

As Paul makes clear in Colossians 3:10 and Ephesians 4:24, Christians are called to 'put off' the old humanity and 'put on' the new humanity, seeking to show those around us a different way of being human, which involves being renewed in Jesus Christ. That renewal extends to the work we do (Colossians 3:22–25; Ephesians 6:5–9), as we work 'with sincerity of heart and reverence for the Lord' (Colossians 3:22). Precisely because we see Jesus 'crowned with glory and honour', we can bear fruit in our daily work, as men and women made and then remade in God's image to represent and reflect the glory of his grace in all the earth.

# 5 Working for Christ

In several of his letters, Paul gives specific exhortations to members of first-century households, including masters and slaves (see also Colossians 3:22–25; Titus 2:9–10; compare 1 Peter 2:18–21). Such households were essentially workplaces, involving growing and preparing food, making furniture, weaving cloth, looking after babies, teaching older children and nursing the sick – with much of this work done by slaves. Slaves had few choices, but they were still part of a human enterprise, contributing to all that nurtured the life of the household.

Paul certainly sees no contradiction in being able to serve Christ as a slave, even saying to the Corinthians: 'Each person should remain in the situation they were in when God called them. Were you a slave when you were called? Don't let it trouble you – although if you can gain your freedom, do so' (1 Corinthians 7:20–21). On the face of it, it looks as though Paul is simply telling slaves to acquiesce to their situation, but underlying his advice here and elsewhere is the reality of their new identity in Christ.

Our union with Christ results in a new way of life which impacts every area of our existence, including work. So, in writing to the Ephesians, Paul asks slaves to obey masters 'just as you would obey Christ' (v. 5), 'as slaves of Christ' (6:6), 'as if you were serving the Lord' (v. 7). Masters, too, are to treat slaves in a way which demonstrates an understanding 'that he who is both their Master and yours is in heaven' (v. 9).

How far can we draw on these instructions in our own working lives? Are they simply irrelevant? Most of us have far more choices than these Christian slaves. We have relative freedom to change jobs, be a whistle-blower, challenge bad practice or join a union. However, we may well know some whose work is very difficult, dealing with unpredictable bosses, impossible targets and incompetent colleagues, but who cannot afford to lose their job. For most of us, work is a mixture of some stresses and some encouragements: satisfaction in achievements, good outcomes and rewarding relationships. But for us too, Paul's encouragement spans the centuries: 'Whatever you do, work at it with all your heart, as working for the Lord, not for human masters' (Colossians 3:23).

# 6 Restored to work

As Christians, we affirm that 'we believe in the resurrection of the body' (from the *Book of Common Prayer*). Even so, there's an all-too-common tendency to imagine that heaven is somewhere above the bright-blue sky, which is where our disembodied souls will go when we die, leaving the world behind. The biblical picture, as we see in this passage and elsewhere in scripture, is that God remains committed to the earth and will one day renew it. Such a renewal will involve not simply a return to the original creation but a transformation of it.

In line with this, an increasing number of theologians have pointed out that our understanding of work has tended to place a lot of weight on the beginning of the biblical story – creation – and not enough emphasis on the end of the story – consummation. To take one example, Darrell Cosden, in *The Heavenly Good of Earthly Work*, argues that work has intrinsic value and that there will be a place for work in the new creation – a view which he hopes will inspire us to seek transformation of the world through our current work.

Even allowing for symbolic language in biblical descriptions of the future, we are told enough to expect a much more active and fulfilling eternity than the more passive pictures we sometimes associate with life beyond the grave. The vision of the future in Isaiah 65:17–25, which is reaffirmed in the closing chapters of the book of Revelation, is one of building houses and cultivating vineyards – reversing the curse of sin recorded in Genesis 3, restoring the enjoyment of the work of our hands, and banishing work's frustration. It's a picture of people fully human without sin's pollution and corruption, and part of that picture is restored work.

Some even suggest that the good work we do now will in some way carry over to the new heavens and the new earth, which gives our current work eternal significance. Whether or not that's the case, we still work in the light of the future restoration to come. To be sure, some things will be radically different – with discontinuities as well as continuities with what went before – but there's every reason to expect that work will not be removed but renewed in the new creation.

# Guidelines

*In nothing has the Church so lost Her hold on reality as in Her failure to understand and respect the secular vocation… How can anyone remain interested in a religion which seems to have no concern with nine-tenths of his life?*

So wrote Dorothy Sayers (1893–1957) in a famous essay entitled 'Why Work?' Given that most adult Christians spend more of their time at their workplace than anywhere else, it's crucial to understand how our faith relates to this significant sphere of life. Our work matters deeply to God. Even when it's challenging, difficult or frustrating, work is a service we offer to Jesus himself (Colossians 3:23). Working for Christ not only gives us a new master, but a new freedom to worship through our work, a new desire to serve others, a new confidence to trust God in our jobs, and a new motivation to work well.

Just one of the ways we can bring our faith and work closer together is through prayer – by bringing our work into our prayer life and prayer into our work life, and by praying for others in their work. For some of us, this could involve a commitment to pray on our commute, or to take a few moments at the start of each day to pray through the items in our diary. Others are helped by regular prompts throughout the day (praying briefly every time the phone rings, or just before entering a room, or when starting a meeting). Still others use the 'prayer of examen', an ancient practice of reflecting on the events of the day in order to discern God's presence and direction. As with other spiritual disciplines, regular habits of prayer shape us over time, in work as in every area of life.

**12–18 February**

# 1 Work and discipleship

**Luke 10:38–42**

What do you do? Often this is the first question we ask of someone when we meet them. It's a way of defining ourselves and others, an indication that we see work as a key part of our identity, which is why unemployment, retirement or extended periods of sickness can hit people hard. Today's passage reminds us that there is value in good work, but that Christians have an even higher source of identity, one found in relationship with Jesus. It's highly unlikely that Jesus is discounting the value of showing hospitality (and the work involved). Luke contains many stories about meals, and hospitality is noted in scripture as a gift and is deeply valued.

More significantly, Mary is portrayed as taking the traditional place of a disciple, seating herself at Jesus' feet to listen and learn. The idea that a woman would learn from a rabbi might well have struck many in the original audience as at least surprising, and perhaps even scandalous. This might also tie in with the immediately preceding passage: the parable of the good Samaritan. Both episodes show how Jesus disrupts the social, ethnic and gender boundaries assumed by the culture in which he lived.

In addition, it may not be Martha's work that is the problem so much as her fussing. Jesus' concern is not primarily with the tasks Martha is absorbed in but with her anxiety over them. This fits with the portrayal of the life of discipleship elsewhere in Luke (e.g. 8:14; 12:22–31). Exhortations not to worry about what we will eat and what we will wear don't remove from us the need to go about making sure we have food and clothes, just as praying for our daily bread (Luke 11:3) doesn't take away the responsibility of sowing the seed, gathering the harvest, making the flour and baking the loaf.

So there may well be a lesson about priorities here, about getting work into proper perspective. Even good things can distract us from essential things. Work is a noble task, but not when it's at the expense of listening to Jesus. While there may be some occupations off limits to Christians, there is no inherent contradiction between working and being a follower of Jesus. But relationship with him comes first.

# 2 Work and laziness

**2 Thessalonians 3:6–15**

It's possible to elevate work to a level that it ought never to have. The tower of Babel incident (Genesis 11:1–9) tells a story of people working for their own glory and personal gain, seeking to make a name for themselves (Genesis 11:4). Using our God-given ability to work with the sole aim of making a name for ourselves or with delusions of grandeur go against the grain of God's purposes for work.

It's worth doing some soul-searching about our own approach to work. There is the danger of succumbing to idolatry, where our job becomes the primary object of our passion and source of our identity. Or we may slide into idleness, unable to see God's purposes in work. Both are problematic, though Paul is dealing with the latter in today's passage.

The issue is laid out in verse 11, when Paul says that some are 'idle and disruptive… not busy [but] busybodies'. Reading between the lines, it sounds like some members of the church community are no longer working and are sponging off other members. It may well be that they had been expecting Jesus' return and so had given up work. Or it could be a result of patron–client relationships, whereby someone of a lower status would attach themselves to a person of higher status in order to benefit from that connection.

Whatever the reason, Paul wants the church to address the situation. His directions seek to maintain the integrity of the community, but also to bring those who are 'idle and disruptive' (v. 6) back into fellowship. Paul's teaching here echoes passages in his earlier letter to this church. His command in 1 Thessalonians 4:11, that they 'lead a quiet life' and 'work with [their] own hands' would seem to forbid Christians playing the part of a client. There, too, Paul uses his own example of working night and day so as not to be a burden to others (1 Thessalonians 2:9; 2 Thessalonians 3:7–9).

There will always be some people out of work through no fault of their own, whether through redundancy or illness or something else. For most of the rest of us, putting it somewhat bluntly, work is not less than an essential means to 'settle down and earn the food [we] eat' (v. 12).

# 3   Wisdom at work

**Proverbs 31:10–31**

With the 'fear of the Lord' as its first principle (Proverbs 1:7), wisdom begins with a deep reverence for God and results in a life of discipline and discernment in every arena of existence, including work. Understood within scripture as a whole, it's no surprise that the book of Proverbs praises the wise for their diligence in work and rebukes the foolish for their negligence.

In particular, set against the slothful worker who appears several times in Proverbs (6:6–11; 12:24; 13:4; 15:19; 21:25; 24:30–34) is the industrious woman from today's passage. In fact, this remarkable portrayal is the Bible's fullest description of the regular activity of an 'ordinary' person – a woman who 'fears the Lord' (v. 30), whose wisdom is demonstrated in her everyday activities. She works wisely in every sphere in which she is involved. Her work embraces her home and family, but extends beyond that to the marketplace (vv. 13–14), with ventures in farming (v. 16), business (v. 18) and manufacturing (v. 19). As well as this, she is careful to look out for those in need (v. 20). In line with Genesis 1, she can be seen as a cultivator of creation, contributing to society through planting and gardening, designing and manufacturing, buying and selling. In addition, it's evident that she works with diligence, compassion, creativity, vision, purpose and love.

In a book which begins with a portrayal of wisdom as a woman inviting people to come to her to receive insight and understanding from God, the woman of Proverbs 31:10–31 is arguably a picture of wisdom itself – and so this image is applicable to men as much as to women. It applies to all because it sets out the ideal of practical wisdom, involving words and deeds, operating in every sphere of life – at home, in the fields, at the city gate (where business deals were struck and lawsuits judged), in the market square – and embracing the daily rhythms of eating, drinking, working and sleeping.

This allows us to pull back the lens and ask what the passage would look like if the woman were a teacher, a mechanic or an accountant. It's also an encouraging reminder that while sin may corrupt God's world, good work can still be carried out in a way that honours God and serves others.

# 4  Work in society

Jeremiah 29:1–14

How should Christians relate to the culture in which they find themselves? One model which has commended itself to many is what sociologist James Davison Hunter has called 'faithful presence'. The exemplar here is Jeremiah 29 – the prophet's letter to the Judean exiles in Babylon, who were living in a very different culture from their true home, yet called on to seek its welfare.

The very ordinariness of Jeremiah's instructions in verses 5–6 may come as a surprise – 'build... settle... plant... eat... marry... have sons and daughters... increase in number'. It's not too difficult to see echoes here of the original mandate given to humanity, the commission to cultivate God's good creation (Genesis 1:28; 2:15). Here, in the sixth century BC, Babylon is a reaffirmation of the significance of embodied, material, family and social life, extended across generations. 'Seek the peace and prosperity of the city,' writes Jeremiah (v. 7). Here, 'peace and prosperity' translate the single Hebrew word *shalom*, the wholeness and well-being that are marks of God's blessing. The active seeking of *shalom* means that our 'faithful presence' is not a passive compliance with the status quo. We seek the welfare of the places we live in through our everyday work, as we're involved in doing business, manufacturing goods, providing services, teaching children, writing reports, designing software, mopping floors, stacking shelves, emptying bins and changing nappies – in different ways, contributing to the success of society.

This being Babylon, there will be dangers – as the book of Daniel makes all too clear. Daniel and his friends bear the cost of being faithful to God. Even so, they do not retreat into a holy enclave. They remain faithful even while taking on pagan names, learning the language and literature of the Babylonians, and serving in the administration of the 'enemy'. They serve the God of Zion, even while seeking the *shalom* of Babylon.

Through it all we live in hope. Jeremiah promises that God will end the exile and restore the Judeans to Jerusalem (vv. 10–14). We too actively pursue *shalom* in our everyday spheres, even as we continue to pray 'Your kingdom come, your will be done, on earth as it is in heaven' (Matthew 6:10), confident that God will one day bring about the restoration of all things.

# 5  Witness at work

1 Thessalonians 4:1–12

It's worth noting the larger collection of Paul's instructions to the Thessalonians on 'how to live in order to please God' (v. 1). The Christian lifestyle is marked by holiness (vv. 3–8) – not just in matters related to sexual relationships, though that is the particular focus here – and by love for others (vv. 9–10). Then comes the specific exhortation about work in verses 11 and 12, which is striking in its mundaneness: 'lead a quiet life… mind your own business and work with your hands… so that your daily life may win the respect of outsiders and so that you will not be dependent on anybody'.

Two important threads run through the whole passage – a 'love for God' and a 'love for neighbour'. Paul lays down the instructions he gave the Thessalonians 'in order to please God' (4:1–2), instructions which reflect 'God's will' (4:3), which were 'taught by God' (4:9). All told, eight times in all, God or Jesus is said to be the ground of these exhortations. But the instructions also shape relationships within and outside the Christian community. They are told not to 'wrong or take advantage' of each other (4:6), 'to love each other' (4:9), and to live and work in such a way 'to win the respect of outsiders' (4:12). In all areas of our Christian walk and witness, love of God and love of neighbour provide the safest and best possible principles.

For us, as for the Thessalonians, we are called to live faithfully not just in the home or at church, but also in the public sphere of work. The sheer amount of time we spend at work means we're more likely to witness to others by how we work as much as by what we say. Holiness does not involve withdrawing from the world of work so much as participating in that world in a new and different way. According to this passage, it's a way which flows out of seeking to live a life that pleases God, within the context of love for fellow believers, and a missional concern for the wider world.

# 6 Rest from work

**Exodus 20:1–17**

Perhaps somewhat curiously, of all the ten commandments, the one devoted to remembering the sabbath takes up the most space (vv. 8–11). The repetition of the command elsewhere (e.g. Exodus 31:12–17), along with the wider principle embodied in laws related to sabbath years and the Jubilee (Leviticus 25), also shows its significance. Its importance is reinforced by being linked to key moments in the biblical story.

First of all, Exodus 20:11 ties the observance of the sabbath to the 'week' of creation, taking us back to Genesis 2:2–3: 'By the seventh day God had finished the work he had been doing; so on the seventh day he rested from all his work. Then God blessed the seventh day and made it holy, because on it he rested from all the work of creating that he had done.' Note the four key verbs: God *finished* the work he was doing; God *rested* from his work; God *blessed* the seventh day; and he *hallowed* the seventh day, setting it apart as special. In doing so, God established a pattern not just for his own people, but for 'any foreigner residing in your towns' (v. 10). The rhythm of work and rest is somehow woven into God's design for all creation.

Then, secondly, the reiteration of the ten commandments in Deuteronomy ties sabbath-keeping to God's redemption of his people from slavery in Egypt (Deuteronomy 5:15). He delivered them from the ceaseless toil of Pharaoh's brick-building system, giving them the freedom to work with dignity and take time off, and the freedom to maintain proper family relationships. Once again, they are instructed to extend that freedom to others.

For those living in the new covenant era, where Jesus is 'Lord of the sabbath' (Matthew 12:8), there is flexibility on what keeping the sabbath might look like in practice. Still, its principles remain crucial and applicable across the board. Perhaps above all, observing the sabbath is an act of trust. Rest recalibrates the market-driven values of our culture. It's a way of saying that this world will run for a while without our input. It involves putting that trust back in the God who graciously and generously provides all things.

## Guidelines

As we have seen in our readings, work is significant from a biblical perspective not because it appears on every page of the Bible, but because it is bound up with the story told throughout the Bible, from beginning to end. It's a story in which God creates all good things – including work. When it goes wrong, God's plan of restoration comes to its climax in Jesus, in whom God will one day bring all things – including work – to their completion.

Those of us in positions of leadership in churches or who preach regularly are ideally placed to show people that God is highly interested in work; that God understands the possibilities and frustrations of work; that God knows the complexities involved in depending on others at work; that God is also concerned about appropriate rhythms of work and rest.

Many church leaders find it beneficial to visit people in their workplace to see where they work, meet their colleagues and pray for them. Some churches have a regular slot when they gather in which someone talks about their work and shares prayer needs. Preaching a one-off sermon series on work might be valuable as an occasional gesture, but members of congregations are arguably best served by an ongoing attitude towards handling scripture which demonstrates awareness of the struggles and opportunities work brings, and which seeks to relate the Bible to those. If we routinely include application to the workplace in sermons and Bible studies, people will begin to see how God, through scripture, equips them for everyday life.

**FURTHER READING**
Robert J . Banks, *God the Worker* (Albatross Books, 1992).
Darrell Cosden, *The Heavenly Good of Earthly Work* (Paternoster, 2006).
James M. Hamilton Jr, *Work and Our Labor in the Lord* (Crossway, 2017).
Timothy Keller, *Every Good Endeavour: Connecting your work to God's plan for the world* (Hodder & Stoughton, 2012).
Tom Nelson, *Work Matters: Connecting Sunday worship to Monday work* (Crossway, 2011).

# The five books of Psalms

There are psalms, and there is the book of Psalms. Usually, whether in a church service or in private times of prayer, we use the psalms individually and in isolation from each other. That the one which starts 'The Lord is my shepherd...' is number 23 is just one of those things and we do not give it a second thought.

While the evidence on which to base wider considerations is not plentiful, there are nevertheless two reasons why it might be worth thinking about Psalms as a complete book. In the first place, it is obvious that somebody wanted us to consider them as some sort of a collection by the fact that the Psalter is divided into five 'books'. The NRSV clearly labels them as such, even though that is not part of the original text. But the comment at the end of Psalm 72 is certainly part of the text of the Bible, as are the little doxologies which conclude and therefore mark out each 'book'. In addition, there are within the Psalter some groups of psalms, such as the Psalms of Asaph (Psalms 72—83) and the Songs of Ascents (Psalms 120—134), which have obviously been collected together. So it is worth asking ourselves whether it is possible to make sense of the order.

Secondly, regardless of how far we go in tracing order in the Psalter, the fact is undeniable that the psalms were finally collected together long after many of the individual psalms had been written. This means that they were valued as religious poetry after the circumstances that first gave rise to them had passed. A psalm about the king when there was no king in Jerusalem cannot mean quite the same as when there was such a king. That we have a book of psalms completed late in the Old Testament period should liberate us from trying to reconstruct how, when or why any given psalm was first written and allow it to give expression, rather, to our own situations and emotional responses as, of course, generations of Jews and Christians have done over the centuries. Remarkably, the fact that there is a Psalter rather than just a collection of psalms helps justify the personal and devotional use for which they have always been so valued.

These notes will focus on the psalms at the beginning and end of each of the five 'books'. Quotations are from the New Revised Standard Version.

# 1  Praying the Bible

We usually think of the psalms as prayers, whether of praise and worship or of lament and petition. That is how many churches use them in their liturgy, and many hymns have been based on them.

This first psalm is not like that, however. It reflects, rather, on two types of people – those who prosper because of devotion to God's word (his 'law', v. 2) and those whose social standing is ephemeral (v. 4) and whose future is insecure (v. 5) because they do not. The two types are then neatly contrasted in the concluding verse.

It is surely not a coincidence that this is the first psalm. The last line of verse 3 echoes Joshua 1:7–8, where Joshua is encouraged to meditate on God's law if he is to prosper. The 'law' in that case is obviously the first five books of the Bible (the Pentateuch or Torah). The book of Psalms is also divided up into five 'books'. It does not take much of a leap of imagination, therefore, to suggest that the author of this psalm wants us to approach the collection that he is introducing as if it too were a word from God. We should read and study it with the same degree of attention that we do any other part of 'the word of God'.

On first reflection that is rather a strange idea. How can a prayer to God suddenly become a word *from* God? This psalm suggests that it can be both at the same time. The psalms were written out of human experience in order to help others articulate joys and anxieties in the presence of God. Over time, those that were found to have lasting appeal were gradually collected for use in temple, synagogue and private worship. So highly valued did this collection become that the author of this present psalm must have come to realise that God had himself been teaching the psalmists to pray, just as Jesus later did his disciples (Luke 11:1–4). A theology that embraces the truth of the incarnation cannot do other than this.

It follows that we in turn are being introduced to a book that encourages us in very different circumstances to pray according to God's will, and at the same time to meditate on the words of the psalms that follow as indicative of God's compassionate love as well as challenging our understanding of the human heart.

# 2 David as Everyman

This psalm has several distinctive features. Firstly it does not have a heading as many of the following psalms do. Given that it is clearly reflecting the words of the Davidic king, it is curious that it is not entitled 'A Psalm of David'. Secondly, the very last line of the psalm sounds like an echo of the first line of Psalm 1. And thirdly, the phrase 'perish in the way' in verse 11 uses the same words as were used of the wicked in the last verse of Psalm 1. If it were not labelled as Psalm 2 in our Bibles, therefore, we might conclude that it was meant to be a continuation of the first psalm.

In substance, of course, it could not be more different. We have to envisage a king in Jerusalem being confronted by rebellious neighbouring states, warning them off their plans to attack by reminding them that he is God's chosen king in Zion, with all the promises of divine protection that this was supposed to entail. (It makes no difference to us as modern readers whether this is a real or an imagined scenario.) In other words, this is a 'psalm of David' *par excellence*, whether 'David' refers to David himself or to one of his descendants. We might suppose, therefore, that it is so far removed from our own situation as to be more or less irrelevant to us. Indeed, as we read on in the Psalter we might come to the same conclusion with many of the psalms of David; their world has no contact with ours.

The person who arranged the book of Psalms is here suggesting a different way of looking at things. If we read Psalm 2 as a sort of continuation of Psalm 1, then it follows that David is being presented as the classic example of the person in Psalm 1:1 who is blessed because of his or her righteousness. In other words, we are all 'David' for the purpose of reading the psalms, so that his words can also be ours. That explains too why the psalm ends with the encouragement that all, not just David, who take refuge in God will be blessed. Taken as a pair, Psalms 1 and 2 thus allow us to accept all the psalms for ourselves; they are not just a private conversation between David and his God.

# 3 A perplexing contrast

**Psalm 41**

This psalm is the last in the first 'book' of the Psalter. The last verse does not really belong to the psalm at all. It is a brief form of doxology that serves to round out the book as a whole; there are similar doxologies concluding each of the books. It may also not be a coincidence that the psalm starts in exactly the same way as Psalm 1, pronouncing a blessing on a certain type of person ('Happy are those who…'). That covers verses 1–3, after which the psalm moves over into more of a direct prayer, introduced by 'I said' in verse 4.

The psalm seems to reflect on one type of righteous person, namely the one who pays particular attention to those less privileged than them, whether materially or in other ways. Rather disconcertingly, the psalmist finds that such a good spirit may evoke adversity, whether in health (v. 3) or more especially among his close contemporaries, as described more fully in the bulk of the psalm (vv. 4–9). While the psalmist confesses in verse 4 that 'I have sinned against you,' the adversity that he now faces is out of proportion with his previous experience of God's grace. While it might be expected from 'enemies', who hardly need any excuse to want to see our end (vv. 5–8), betrayal by our closest companion is almost unintelligible (v. 9).

The language of the psalms is quite often elusive like this, and I am of the opinion that this is deliberate. As with all great poetry, readers often want to go behind the text of the Psalms to uncover the story that gave rise to the composition. But that is not why poetry is usually written and published. However much it may or may not reflect the poet's personal experience, each reader may, within reason, make of it what fits with his or her own experience. So too with a psalm such as this one. It becomes a vehicle for giving expression to our deepest frustrations, quite different though these may be for each one of us, and allows us to do so in the confidence that in God's sight the care for the disadvantaged is an overwhelming priority that merits his blessing (v. 1). It will also lead ultimately to our vindication in his sight, even if not in the sight of others (vv. 10–12).

# 4  God as hope and help

These two psalms are in fact just one, as the repeated refrain in 42:5, 11, and 43:5 makes clear.

The second book of the Psalter begins with an expression of passionate longing for renewed participation in congregational worship at the temple. The psalmist wistfully remembers his joy on previous visits (see especially 42:4), but for some reason that is not entirely clear to us he is now prevented from coming. With a kaleidoscope of telling images, he expresses his despair at this: he is like a parched young deer thirsting for refreshing water (42:1); he feels as though he is drowning in a flood that has swept over him (42:7); the words of those who taunt him because God is not helping him are like mortal wounds in his body (see the repeated question in 42:3, 10). Such imagery cannot be harmonised into a single picture. In its variety, it explores ways of giving voice to otherwise inexpressible despair.

This very variety opens a door for us also to enter into the world of the psalm. Most of us have enjoyed times of rich worship in fellowship with others, and equally most of us have experienced periods of alienation from that, when we long to have the former joy restored. We can use the imagery of the psalm to express our own sense of longing. At the root of it all, however, is the lurking fear that somehow God himself is implicated in the problem – that not just 'enemies' but even God has 'cast me off' (43:2). But past experience shows that this cannot be the final word, and so the refrain repeatedly challenges the psalmist's sense of despair with the assured hope that he will once again be restored to a life of praise.

This book of Psalms thus opens with a realistic diagnosis of our condition. We long to be able to join with others in using these prayers and praises, but frankly we do not always feel like it. The psalm encourages us to look away from permanent morbid introspection and to focus instead upon the God who alone is our hope and our help.

# 5 Hail to the Lord's anointed

Verses 18–19 are the doxology that concludes the second book of the Psalter, and it is followed by a comment that this is also the end of the prayers of David (even though there are in fact a few more psalms attributed to David later on). This may indicate that the Psalter developed over a long period of time, though we cannot now retrace all the steps in that process.

This psalm is in any case a great way to bring such a collection to a conclusion. It is a prayer for the king. Two of its four parts (vv. 1–7 and 12–14) request that he will fulfil within his own national society his highest duty of ensuring that justice in all its dimensions will be executed without fear or favour. He might be the only bastion of support for those whose circumstances leave them open to exploitation by others more wealthy and powerful than they. When those with the highest privileges give themselves to the well-being of those at the bottom of the pile, all may share plentifully in the bounty of the natural world which God alone can control.

Verses 8–11 and 15–17, by contrast, look outwards towards the king's reputation on the international scene. While there are typical expressions of the hope that he will 'have dominion' (v. 8) over his enemies, there is also, in verse 17, a clear indication that his good reputation and standing will lead also to the blessing of 'all nations' (v. 11). Again, privilege is not just for personal enjoyment but an avenue through which God acts for the good of others.

The Christian church typically uses paraphrases of this psalm as an appropriate way to extol the supreme example of Jesus Christ in all these regards. But just as we are all 'David' as we read the psalms, so too we need to recall that Christ was an example for us even while doing unique things that we could not do for ourselves. Just as we 'hear' this psalm as part of God's word, so we should also pray through it for its impact on our own personal and societal scale of values.

# 6  Regaining perspective

The third book of the Psalter begins with a psalm that is as much meditation as prayer. If we had read all the psalms consecutively up until this point, we might have encountered a dilemma. There are psalms which boldly proclaim God's might and goodness; there are others (perhaps even a majority) which lament that the world is not as it should be, and the psalmist seems always to be the one who is suffering the consequences.

This dilemma is explored here in verses 1–14. Those who live without reference to God often seem to prosper, not only economically but also in their social standing and sense of self-esteem. It makes the psalmist envious and tempted to backslide. The orthodox sentiment of verse 1 is contradicted by personal experience (v. 2). So what's the point of trying to live a godly and pure life (vv. 13–14)?

The initial response is in danger of sounding trite: it will all turn out all right if you go to church (v. 17). Of course, that needs some unpacking, and the main point that the psalmist wants to get across is the fact that our values in life are inevitably determined by our overall sense of perspective (vv. 18–28). Part of this involves taking a long-term view of things and seeing the eventual outcome of the two contrasting lifestyles: ruin or an eternity with God.

But 'pie in the sky' is rarely the Old Testament's solution to life's conundrums, and here too it is not where the emphasis lies. Rather, the psalmist reorientates his sense of values in the light of worship, with its recalling of God's past acts of deliverance and its expressions of confident trust for the future. In that light he comes back to the realisation that life with God, who is his refuge and strength even when circumstances seem to belie it, is inherently 'right'; to follow the alternative path, however outwardly attractive, is 'stupid and ignorant' (v. 22).

A perspective in which God's values are appreciated more than personal gain needs constant renewal, and corporate worship is one sure way to help with that. We are all tempted to adopt different values, and we can see the extent to which the modern world is shaped accordingly. Reading and praying this psalm can help us maintain a sense of values shaped by an ultimate rather than ephemeral perspective.

# Guidelines

Many of the psalms, including some we have read this week, include sentiments with which we today find it difficult to sympathise. Sometimes the psalmist seems to have a higher idea of himself than we think decent; on other occasions, the way enemies are described and their downfall anticipated does not sound very Christian. Can we, then, use such prayers with integrity?

Of course, we have to recognise that we do not know the circumstances in which these psalms were originally written. Many books are written to try to tie down these questions in a historical manner, but nothing is certain. More importantly, the precise circumstances would soon have been forgotten as these prayers became the property of the worshipping community in the temple and in the synagogue. They come to us, therefore, not as part of the psalmist's autobiography but as prayers which were found sufficiently helpful to be preserved in the life of the worshipping community. It is a bit like hymns: hundreds are written and for a short while may be appreciated. But only a few survive for more than a decade or two and become part of the classic stock which have to feature in any self-respecting hymn book.

As we read and use the psalms today, therefore, we should not feel embarrassed about interpreting them in the ways with which we are most comfortable. Those ways too will vary as we go through differing life experiences. As you pray a psalm, allow its imagery to give expression to the sentiments you feel at that time, whether joyful or angry or depressed. The words that come to us from so long ago can help to give expression to us exactly where we are, and to turn us from that situation towards the God who is able to conform us more and more into the image he would like us to share.

O Lord, hear our prayers, not according to the poverty of our asking but according to the riches of your grace, so that our lives may conform to those desires which accord with your will; through Jesus Christ our Lord. Amen

# 1 How long, O Lord?

**Psalm 89**

It all starts out so well. The first three-quarters of this psalm sound like unqualified exuberant praise. As creator, God is king of the universe without rival. He has subdued chaos in order to establish a stable world, founded on principles of justice and righteousness (vv. 5–18). The psalmist sings of God's faithfulness and steadfast love (vv. 1–2).

More than that, in his providential ordering of this good world, God has installed a human deputy to care for his people (vv. 3–4, 19–37). He has promised never to abandon the Davidic king and to ensure that he will be victorious over his enemies. Even if a particular king may need to be judged for faithlessness, that will only be temporary (vv. 30–33). The underlying promise that the Davidic line will never fail remains immutable (vv. 28–29, 34–37).

Suddenly, however, we discover in the closing verses (38–51) that this has all gone horribly wrong, that every element of the promise seems to have been broken. The psalmist cannot understand how or why God has not acted in the way that he said he would. Is this a final judgement (v. 46)? Where is that steadfast love from which the psalm started out in praise (v. 49)? These questions remain unresolved at the end of the psalm.

We do not know whether this psalm was a response to the final fall of the monarchy or whether it reflects some earlier crisis. However, it continued to be valued and was included in the Psalter in the centuries when there certainly was no king in Jerusalem. It gives meaningful expression to the despair which all believers experience at one time or another, that there is a mismatch between what God seems to promise in the Bible and the realities of current experience. It allows us to voice our frustrations – not to pretend that things are other than they are but actually to tell God that this really is not good enough. And in that, we show that even in despair there remains the faith born of past experience that we can still approach God with integrity; he is not some malevolent force of whom we should live in constant terror, but the God and Father of our Lord Jesus Christ who came to make good on God's promise in a way that far exceeded anything that the ancient psalmist could have envisaged.

# 2  They are soon gone

Most of this psalm that opens the fourth book of the Psalter is an extended (and deeply moving) meditation on human mortality. Compared with God's eternity, life is brief and therefore in danger of being judged inconsequential – an observation which modern scientific understanding of the history of the universe makes even more poignant than the ancient psalmist could have imagined. Several of the varied images which the psalmist uses to express this contrast have entered common English parlance, which is an indication of their transparency and effectiveness.

Part of the dilemma is attributed to God's anger and wrath (vv. 7, 9 and 11). Although there is one brief mention of sin (v. 8), this does not seem to furnish a satisfactory explanation of the basic issue; after all, there is no hint here that a better life would lead to immortality. I therefore think we have to ascribe it to human perception rather than to sound theology, somewhat like people today who respond to difficulty by saying, 'What have I done to deserve this?' When faced with real perplexity, we try to explain things to ourselves in words and categories with which we are familiar.

In fact, the psalmist indicates in other parts of the psalm that he is aware of alternatives. He knows that God shows compassion (v. 13), is characterised by the quality of steadfast love (v. 14) and can give significance to what people do even in the brief allotted span of life (v. 17). In this way the meditation on mortality is set in a framework of proper acknowledgement of God's everlasting beneficent nature (vv. 1–2) and responsive prayer that he will soon act in accordance with his true character ('in the morning' vv. 13–17).

The paraphrase of this psalm ('O God, our help in ages past') has in English-speaking churches become a standard hymn in times of remembrance for those lost in war. Has hymn writer Isaac Watts distorted the psalmist's sense of despair, or has he appropriately transferred the acute sense of God's wrath in relation to human mortality to the setting of armed conflict in the modern world?

# 3  History's vicissitudes

**Psalm 106**

The fourth book of the Psalter began in a subdued, if not depressed, mood, but it moves steadily in a more positive direction. Psalms 93 and 95—100 rejoice in God as king, the founder of justice and righteousness, while Psalms 103 and 104 each start, 'Bless the Lord, O my soul.' The book then concludes with two lengthy psalms, including this one, that trace some highlights of God's involvement in Israel's history. These remind us, perhaps, that worship is not always abstract – in contrast with praising God for things like his kingship that are outside of our daily experience – nor is it restricted to thanks for his regular provision for our physical needs as creator. It must also include our experience of his involvement in the daily hardships of life.

Broadly speaking, Psalm 105 recalls God's past dealings with his people in very positive terms. With references to the stories we now find in Genesis and Exodus, it focuses on God's gracious provision of his people's varying needs in widely differing circumstances. Psalm 106 is almost like a mirror image of Psalm 105. It starts in Exodus, so to speak (vv. 7–23), and moves further forward into Numbers (vv. 24–33) and some of the later historical books which deal with Israel's life in the promised land (from v. 34 on), but in this account the focus is on the people's sin, rebellion and rejection of God's direction.

It is not so much a confession (despite v. 6) as a narrative account of how even in these negative circumstances God always moved either on his own initiative (for example, vv. 8–12 and 43–46) or by raising up one who would deliver the people on his behalf (Moses in v. 23 and Phinehas in v. 30). Because of these past experiences of the steadfast love of God in the teeth of rebellion, the psalmist is emboldened to pray that he will continue to act as he has in the past (v. 47) and that he himself may as an individual be included within this (vv. 4–5).

Life is seldom tidy, nor is our response to its ups and downs. This encourages us to appreciate that God is not bound by our failures and lack of consistent faith but operates rather in conformity with his own very different character; he will not be deflected by our inadequacies. No wonder the psalmist could conclude this book with another doxology (v. 48)!

# 4 Then they cried to the Lord

**Psalm 107**

This first psalm of the fifth book has many points of contact with Psalms 105 and 106 (note, for instance, how similar the first verse in each is). This suggests that they once belonged together and that the division of the Psalter into five books was quite a late development.

Whereas the two previous psalms deal with recognisable events in Israel's history, this one concentrates more on general (albeit sometimes quite extreme) circumstances in daily life. Nevertheless, verse 3 in the introduction and the more generalising concluding section in verses 33–43 sound as though the psalmist may have the restoration of the people in the Babylonian exile especially in mind; parts of these verses sound very like the prophecies of restoration in Isaiah 40—55. So perhaps the individual acts of deliverance which are recalled in the bulk of the psalm are also meant to be illustrative of that great act of deliverance. In verses 4–32, four scenarios of human distress are depicted, from each of which the afflicted appealed to God and he delivered them; they are therefore invited to give thanks and praise.

In the church I attend, during the evening service on Harvest Thanksgiving Sunday, two local fishermen bring their nets to the chancel for thanks and a blessing while verses 23–32 are read, and then, of course, we sing a hymn about 'those in peril on the sea'. But the lifeboat crew are also there, and all around our small town there are vivid reminders of the number of wrecks that our coastline has witnessed over the years. It is sometimes difficult to harmonise the praise of this psalm with the experience of those who have cried to the Lord and yet not been delivered.

There is no simple answer to this dichotomy. The end of the exile in Babylon did not work out as gloriously as the prophecies might have led people to expect but, even so, 'those who are wise' (v. 43) still find here a reflection of God's steadfast love. In our very different circumstances we too are invited to pause, reflect and try to discern God's loving purposes as experienced by some as a foretaste of their fuller and eternal endurance (v. 1). Sometimes communal testimony and worship are able to put uncertainty into a wider perspective.

# 5  Songs of ascents

The fifth book of the Psalter is long, and some commentators think that Psalm 119 marks a break in it. What is more, Psalms 120—134, which immediately follow it, are all titled 'A Song of Ascents', so it looks as though they are an earlier collection which has been included here. Perhaps we may therefore pause to look at them as well.

These psalms, several of which seem to be many people's favourites, are mostly quite short, and many of them imply that they have been collected to serve as a resource for pilgrims on their way to Jerusalem for one of the major festivals. Alternatively, it has sometimes been suggested that they were sung by the Levites, one on each of the 15 steps up into the temple courtyard.

Psalm 121 may obviously have been inspired by reflection on the potential dangers encountered on a long journey through open countryside and confronting the steep climb up from the Jordan Valley through the Judean hills. Exposure by day and risks of other sorts by night are allayed by meditation on the Lord as the traveller's keeper and guardian. It is not surprising that by way of imaginative reapplication this simple but elegant psalm has been found to reassure believers in the widest possible variety of other threatening circumstances. There is no need to try to be clever to find anything more here than the simple reassurance that it offers to anyone whose faith allows them to say that their help ultimately comes not from any manner of human devising, but from the Lord.

Psalm 122 combines excitement at the prospect of pilgrimage to Jerusalem with anxiety for its peace and welfare. It was a journey that many had travelled previously, so it was undertaken with a strong sense of tradition. Jerusalem was both a worship and an administrative centre (vv. 3–5), so it gave reassurance to be on the way there again. The 'peace of Jerusalem', for which all are encouraged to pray (vv. 6–7), is not just absence of war but total well-being. It is a prayer that we might well offer still for the physical Jerusalem of today, but surely also for the church, both local and universal; where else can pilgrim souls find the divine solace that they seek? If the church is divided or otherwise out of sorts, its witness is tarnished.

# 6 Praise the Lord!

**Psalm 150**

We have noted that each of the first four books of the Psalter ends with a little doxology. The fifth book, and so the Psalter as a whole, however, ends not just with a verse or two tacked on to the previous psalm but with a complete psalm of praise all of its own. And what an exuberant psalm it is! Suffice to observe here that every verse in the NRSV ends with an exclamation mark, as do several of the intermediate lines as well.

In the first two verses, we find a brief summary of every motivation for praise that has been given in more extended fashion in other psalms of praise in the Psalter: God is to be praised as creator, hence the reference to the 'mighty firmament' (v. 1); as the one who undertakes 'mighty deeds' (v. 2), including especially deliverance; and simply because of who he is in himself ('his surpassing greatness', v. 2).

While naturally praise can be offered anywhere, it is obviously especially appropriate in the case of this temple hymn book that it should be offered 'in [the] sanctuary' (v. 1). This fits well with the second half of the psalm, where the music and liturgical movements can clearly only be undertaken corporately. We would probably express praise differently in our own churches from how it is envisaged here. Some would love it, but many would not! What matters, of course, is not the precise style or form of worship so much as the emphatic avowal that the last words of the Psalter are a call to praise. Taken as a whole, the Psalter accompanies us through the whole range of human experience and emotion, from vicious anger and the depths of despair to considered reflection on the past goodness of God in his dealings with his people and acknowledgement of his kingship and sovereignty. The journey, however, is neither random nor circular but has a destination: 'Let everything that breathes praise the Lord!' (v.6).

# Guidelines

In the psalms that have been selected for the past two weeks we have looked at what might be called the 'hinges' of the Psalter – the first and last psalms of each of the five books. They are quite varied in style and mood, and ways have been suggested in which we can appropriate these for our own use. More than that, however, we have tried also to consider them as part of scripture, as a means whereby God communicates something about himself to us as well as a means whereby we address him. I admit that this double way of looking at things can at first be a bit confusing.

Nevertheless, it is well worth developing the habit of studying the psalms as well as saying or singing them in prayer or worship. So often the way we are taught about God and his dealings with the world is unrealistically divorced from how we feel on a Monday morning, when ill in bed, or in a relationship that has gone wrong. You can never say that about the psalms, however. The extremes of emotion to which they give poetic voice mean that we join hands across the generations with the writers of old. Their honesty, which nevertheless eventuates in praise, needs to be built into our whole understanding of the faith.

A Gaelic prayer:

As the rain hides the stars, as the autumn mist hides the hills, as the clouds veil the blue of the sky, so the dark happenings of my lot hide the shining of your face from me. Yet, if I may hold your hand in the darkness, it is enough. Since I know that, though I may stumble in my going, you do not fall.

---

**FURTHER READING**

John Eaton, *The Psalms: A historical and spiritual commentary with an introduction and new translation* (T & T Clark International, 2003).

John Goldingay, *Psalms* (three volumes) (Baker Academic, 2008).

Henry Wansbrough, *The Psalms: A commentary for prayer and reflection* (BRF, 2014).

# Adoption in the Bible

As I write this introduction, it is National Adoption Week in the UK, a concentrated few days when people's newspapers and Facebook feeds fill with articles on the joys and challenges of adoption, and stories of families who have permanently welcomed a child into their home.

Such stories may be easily missed, however, if we are not tuned into the topic, and I wonder if this can be the case with our Bible reading as well. The purpose of this week's studies is to alert us to examples of adoption imagery in God's word, and to see how the biblical writers explored this rich theme. Thinking about the Bible and adoption can take us in a number of directions, two of which we will pursue over the next few days.

Firstly, we will look at stories of adoption in the Bible. While we should be careful when drawing parallels between what happened in biblical times and what happens in our own, there are cases in scripture where a child is taken in by a household and becomes a member of that family.

Secondly, we will focus on how the Bible uses the language of adoption to describe God's relationship with his people. While this is well known of Paul's writings, perhaps it is less recognised as something that happens in the Old Testament.

I hope this will make for an interesting series of studies, but I hope too that the studies will raise the question of how our identity as God's adoptive children will encourage us to look outwards to consider the plight of vulnerable children in our midst. Historically the church has done great things to address the needs of vulnerable children, yet with nearly 70,000 children in the UK care system there is still so much to do. Adoptive families are needed, but so are foster families, as well as churches that work hard to know how to become the best supportive communities they can be.

How can the church respond? How can the Bible shape that response? Perhaps one step we can take is to renew our understanding of our own transforming adoptive identity in God, the roots of which are traced in these studies.

Quotations are from the New Revised Standard Version.

# 1 Moses

Our first look at adoption in the Bible brings us to the early life of Moses. In the opening chapter of Exodus, a dark picture is painted of Israel's circumstances. The warm welcome extended to them generations before has now given way to oppression and enslavement at the hands of the Egyptian Pharaoh. So threatened is he by their growing population that he orders the death of all Israelite male babies. It was into this desperate situation that Moses was born.

The story includes some subtle connections with the book of Genesis. Moses' mother 'saw' that her new baby boy was 'good' (v. 2), perhaps echoing the repeated refrain in Genesis 1 when God 'saw' that his creation was 'good' (see Genesis 1:4, 10, 12, 18, 21, 25, 31). Also, the same Hebrew word is used for Moses' 'basket' as for Noah's 'ark', both vessels providing a means of salvation for their occupants, which will have implications for the whole of humanity (for more details, see commentaries by Peter Enns and James Bruckner). Perhaps, then, these connections are there to help us anticipate a new creative work of God, a great and good work of salvation emerging from the dark chaos of Egyptian oppression.

It isn't clear what Moses' mother expected to happen by putting him in the basket on the river. Nevertheless, he is discovered – by Pharaoh's daughter, no less – and rescued. Add in some quick thinking by his big sister and Moses' life is transformed.

It is impossible to miss the irony of what happens in verses 5–10. The daughter of the one who is oppressing and killing the Israelites has compassion on and rescues their future leader and liberator. Moses' mother had let him go but now she has him back (albeit temporarily), protected and even paid for.

Blending themes of heartbreak, vulnerability, transformation and hope, at the heart of this critical moment in the biblical story, woven into its DNA, is an adoption.

Reflecting on this story, Krish and Miriam Kandiah leave us with a powerful challenge: 'Our ears must be open to the cry of those in distress. Even a pagan princess could not ignore a helpless cry… If even the daughter of the enemy can show this kind of commitment and compassion, then no less is expected of God's people' (*Home for Good*, p. 36).

# 2 An adopted king

**2 Samuel 7:1–17**

Moving on from a human story of adoption, we now see the theme appear in a very different context. Here we find adoption language at a crucial point in the story of David and, indeed, the story of Israel. Now settled in Jerusalem, the king had brought the ark of the covenant to the city as well. David wants to build a 'house' for God in which the ark could be placed. Instead, Nathan the prophet passes on to him a message that God has more in store for the king, including making his name great and establishing his people in the land in peace (vv. 4–11a). Then comes the focal point of today's study in verses 11b–17.

Antony F. Campbell nicely sums up God's response to David's request: 'You will not build a house for me; I will build a house for you' (p. 72). God promises to establish David's descendants as a royal line in perpetuity (vv. 12–13). In verse 14 God declares, 'I will be to him a father, and he shall be to me a son.' At the heart of the Davidic covenant is an adoptive relationship between God and the anointed Davidic king. It is one of privilege but one of responsibility as well (vv. 14–16).

In his article 'Adoption in the Bible' (in *The Child in the Bible* ed. Marcia J. Bunge), David Bartlett is helpful in teasing this out. It is as if God is assuring David that, once he has died, God will take over as Solomon's father, thereby assuring the Davidic line of its kingly inheritance.

The idea of Israel's king as God's adoptive son is expressed elsewhere. In Psalm 2:7, for example, God says to his anointed king, 'You are my son; today I have begotten you.' This seems to be a declaration using the language of formal adoption, again with the assurance of inheritance as a key component. We might remember, as well, that the early church also picked up on this passage when reflecting on the sonship of King Jesus (compare Acts 13:33; Hebrews 1:5; 5:5). And, of course, the report of Jesus' baptism (Mark 1:9–11) resonates as well. The language of adoption, therefore, is woven into the thought world of Israel, and provides an important way of understanding God's promises moving on into the future.

# 3 An adopted people

**Hosea 11:1–11**

Despite yesterday's focus on David's line, the adoptive relationship wasn't the sole preserve of Israel's kings. There was also a sense in which the people of Israel as a whole were depicted as adopted by God.

We gain a glimpse of this in a well-known oracle in Hosea 11, which captures something of the vulnerability, privilege, pain and hope of this powerful relational imagery.

The language of 'call' and 'love' in verse 1 has Old Testament resonances with commitment, election and adoption, which are closely associated in Deuteronomy, a book that seems to be in the background in Hosea (e.g. Deuteronomy 7:6–8; 14:1; see also Douglas Stuart, *Hosea–Jonah*, p. 179; and also Janet Melnyk's important article 'When Israel Was a Child' in *History and Interpretation* ed. M. Patrick Graham et al).

In Hosea 11, we gain an insight into the pain God felt when considering the rebellion of his adoptive child, Israel. Regardless of the privilege of being called and loved by God, Israel chose to reject him (vv. 1–2) despite the nurture they received in God's tender and attentive care (vv. 3–4). Like all children they are subject to consequences if they disobey (vv. 5–7). Yet what is a parent supposed to do? In verses 8–11 God declares that he will not go through with their deserved destruction. Instead Israel will be restored.

We are used, I think, to understanding the people of God since New Testament times as being his children. Think, for example, of John's use of birth imagery in his Gospel (John 1:12–13; 3:4–8). As we will see, especially in the final two studies, Paul also used parent–child language explicitly in his writings. But here it is in the Old Testament as well, albeit more subtly done. God has adopted these people as his children. Indeed, as Janet Melnyk suggests, adoption is the norm for understanding this parental relationship.

# 4 Jesus as adopted

**Matthew 1:18–25**

Joseph seems to be the unsung hero of the story of Jesus' birth. As Russell Moore points out half-jokingly in his book *Adoption*, in school nativity plays sometimes the cows have more lines than the carpenter. The verses in today's passage are well known but perhaps that familiarity leads us to miss the quiet and startling drama of Joseph's part in the story.

What was he supposed to do on hearing that his future bride was pregnant? Being a just man, it seemed to Joseph that probably the best (perhaps only?) decent course of action was to end the relationship, but to do so in a way that didn't humiliate Mary.

We then read an account of a pivotal moment in the story. Joseph is visited in a dream by an angel who tells him of the remarkable origins and purpose of Mary's baby. What's more, the angel charges Joseph with going ahead with the marriage and becoming, in effect, the baby's adoptive father. It could be, suggests David Bartlett in *Adoption in the Bible*, that this passage has echoes of Old Testament adoption language to show how Jesus has now been adopted into the Davidic line, a necessary qualification for the Messiah. This seems persuasive but we shouldn't miss the more human theme present in the story – that is, Joseph's intense vulnerability. Perhaps, following this meeting Joseph didn't really have a choice; after all, how could he turn his back on an angelic visitation? Yet he still had to follow through in front of a watching world that wouldn't have understood what he was doing.

Matthew goes on, in 2:13–15, to recount this vulnerable family's flight to Egypt as they seek to escape the sentence of death hanging over the child.

Our Lord Jesus was himself an adoptee and a child refugee. This was, of course, a unique situation and there are ways in which the nature of this adoption cannot be paralleled. Nevertheless, it seems significant that at the heart of the incarnation is the decision of a man to become the father of a child that was not his, and to enter into a family situation of great risk and vulnerability. Because we know the end of the story, we sometimes gloss over what a precarious situation this was, in human terms at least. Yet this is how God chose to enter our world.

## 5 Paul and adoption (part 1)

**Galatians 4:1–7**

In our final two studies we move on to the theme of adoption as it was used by the apostle Paul. The apostle's first-century Greco-Roman context gave him further layers to work with when reflecting on the adoption theme. It was common for adoption to be used to carry on the family line but, more than this, David Bartlett suggests in *Adoption in the Bible* that it could have been used as a way of maintaining political, social and financial security for parent and child. Paul also had a Greek word for 'adoption' at his disposal. For him, the notion of adoption provided a powerful image with which to explore the good news of the gospel.

Paul's strategy in this passage is to remind the believers at the church in Galatia that they have experienced, by the grace of God, a transformation of their identity. How could they, therefore, abandon God's grace and reject the gospel that has been preached to them (1:6–9)?

In 4:1–7 Paul uses the language of children, heirs, slaves and adoption. The Galatians had been in one state, enslaved and under the law (vv. 3–4), yet now they have been redeemed and adopted into God's family (v. 5)!

In his article, David Bartlett highlights three reflections from Paul's use of adoption imagery here, and I think they are worth considering. Firstly, the gift of the Holy Spirit, who enables us to say, 'Abba! Father!', gives proof of our adoption (v. 6). This is a sure and certain status. Secondly, as we have seen from the use of adoption language in the Old Testament, adoption assures us of an inheritance with God (v. 7). We might say that this guarantees us of a sure and certain future. Finally, adoption transforms not just our prospects but our very identity. In the verses immediately preceding today's passage, Paul declares that we are 'children of God' and part of a new community (indeed, a family) of faith where there is no superiority or inferiority (3:25–29).

No wonder Paul sought to engage with this rich metaphor of adoption for exploring the gospel and its implications for believers. As we've seen, it shines a light on a number of important aspects of our life in Christ. We will see more of this tomorrow in another of Paul's letters, this time to the Romans.

# 6 Paul and adoption (part 2)

**Romans 8:12–17**

Having surveyed the range of the gospel in the preceding chapters of Romans, from the terrible consequences of sin to the glorious forgiveness found in Jesus Christ, Paul now contemplates the life of the believer in a world that is still marked by rebellion against God. What resources do we have as believers for keeping faithful in the midst of hostility?

Those who are in Christ, declares Paul, have been given the life-giving Spirit, the same Spirit who raised Jesus from the dead (8:1, 10–11). And this life-giving Spirit testifies that we are children of God. This welcome into God's family is because of the 'Spirit of adoption' that enables us to cry out to God in the most familiar of ways: 'Abba! Father!' (v. 15).

Again we see themes of identity, assurance and inheritance in Paul's use of adoption imagery. Note also the present-yet-future reality of this adoption. Just as creation has been groaning 'in the pains of childbirth until now' (v. 22), we too 'groan inwardly as we wait eagerly for adoption as sons, the redemption of our bodies' (v. 23).

Returning to the main part of our passage, we should note also the way this adoption is tied closely to Jesus, and what it says about future hope and the nature of the waiting: 'the fruit of adoption is an inheritance. Christians share this inheritance with their firstborn brother, Jesus. And their inheritance, like his, is an inheritance both of suffering and of glory. Suffering and glory are what you get when you are adopted into this particular family' (David Bartlett, *Adoption in the Bible*, p. 391).

Of course, the prospect of suffering is not a comfortable one, either for Paul's original audience or for contemporary readers. Yet it is realistic. Being adopted into God's family means following the way of the cross. But being adopted by God also means being an heir to all of his resourcing and promises. Finally, Paul's magisterial chapter ends with the confident declaration that the family bonds will not be broken, that nothing 'will be able to separate us from the love of God in Christ Jesus our Lord' (v. 39).

## Guidelines

In this short series we have seen a variety of ways in which adoption features in the Bible, and have caught a glimpse of the richness of this biblical image. We have looked at the story of an adoption in the Old Testament, and we have witnessed God's adoptive relationship with the people of Israel in general, and with the Davidic king in particular.

Moving into the New Testament we paused to consider the adoptive relationship shared between Joseph and Jesus, before finishing up in Paul's letters to consider his profound understanding of what it means to be adopted into God's family. Adoption, it seems, provided the biblical writers with deep wells from which to draw.

But what are the practical implications of what we have seen? Let me note just a couple of possibilities (among many).

Firstly, a clearer picture of our adoption into God's family should have a transformative effect on how those of us within Christian communities see ourselves and each other. We share an adoption into the same family.

Secondly, adoption in the Bible is no mere private matter. Our 'spiritual adoption' should have a societal resonance, giving the church a transforming vision, a lens through which to view the marginalised around us. Aligned with the consistent biblical call to care for the 'orphan', the adoption theme opens up a way to engage with issues concerning vulnerable children. Part of that whole-church response might be fostering and adoption. If you want to explore this further, I recommend the charity Home for Good (**www. homeforgood.org.uk**). Their website has a number of very practical suggestions for those wanting to support foster carers and adopters in churches.

I conclude with a question from Home for Good's founder, Krish Kandiah: 'What if we the Church could be known as the people who truly care about the pain and problems of children who have no other family to turn to and whom, it seems, nobody wants? What if the Church was known as the most compassionate and hospitable family in the country?' (*Home for Good*, p. 4).

Wouldn't that be a wonderful expression of the family transformation we received when God adopted us?

---

**FURTHER READING**

David L. Bartlett, 'Adoption in the Bible', in Marcia J. Bunge (ed.), *The Child in the Bible* (Eerdmans, 2008), pp. 375–98.

James Bruckner, *Exodus* (Paternoster, 2008).

Antony F. Campbell, *2 Samuel* (Eerdmans, 2005).

Peter Enns, *Exodus* (Zondervan, 2000).

Krish Kandiah with Miriam Kandiah, *Home for Good* (Hodder & Stoughton, 2013).

Janet Melnyk, 'When Israel Was a Child: Ancient Near-Eastern adoption formulas and the relationship between God and Israel', in M. Patrick Graham et al. (eds) *History and Interpretation* (Sheffield Academic Press, 1993), pp. 245–59.

Russell Moore, *Adoption: What Joseph of Nazareth can teach us about this countercultural choice* (Crossway, 2015).

Douglas Stuart, *Hosea–Jonah* (Thomas Nelson, 1987).

# Jesus' parables

The parables of Jesus have stood the test of time and are some of the best-known words in the Bible. There is the good Samaritan, the prodigal son, the sower, the sheep and the goats, and the cursed fig tree. Jesus was a master storyteller and a master teacher. The evangelists learned from his style and, in their own way, composed the stories of Jesus' life, death and resurrection.

Jesus is often quoted as saying, 'Whoever has ears, let them hear' (Matthew 11:15; Mark 7:16 and so on), and this is also used in Revelation (2:29) as a challenge to the churches. Surely the very nature of Jesus' great commission (Matthew 28:16–20) is to disciple those who will listen. Over and over again, the prophets encourage the people to listen to the voice of God: 'It is the Lord who speaks!' The ten commandments start with 'Hear, O Israel…' (Deuteronomy 5:1), which is again a call to listen.

Perhaps it is part of human nature to not actively listen; however, the problem increases when we do not actively listen to the word of God. We miss out on our 'daily bread', our food for the journey, and when we are not well fed, like a tree we do not produce fruit.

This fruit is for the benefit of others; it is our part in the creation story, our part of living in the kingdom of God. Our challenge today is to really listen to the parables and allow them to speak to us anew, feed us and enable us to produce fruit.

Quotations are from the New Revised Standard Version.

## 1 The play within the play

**Matthew 13:10–17**

What should we do with this text? What does Jesus mean when he says that to the general populace he speaks in parables? Is he deliberately hiding secrets or are the crowd simply incapable of understanding them? Does he want everybody to know the truth or just his small group of disciples?

Some writers suggest that Jesus needs to be misunderstood by the crowds in order that his sacrifice may occur. This seems flawed to me because he is crucified due to his claims. The crowds understand what Jesus is saying but refuse to accept it.

Others argue that it is simply a hard heart or spiritual blindness that prevents people from understanding Jesus and fully responding to him. On the whole, the parables are not complicated but the full impact of them can often lead to a change in people's lives – a metanoia response. This is a response similar to that demanded by prophets like Jeremiah (4:1–2), Hosea (14:1–2) and John the Baptist (Matthew 3:1–2).

It's like the play within the play in *Hamlet*: 'The play's the thing wherein I'll catch the conscience of the king,' says Hamlet (Act 2, Scene 2). When Claudius (the king) watches *The Murder of Gonzago* (the play) he comes face-to-face with his own life and actions, leading to a response. So it is with Jesus' parables. Jesus tells stories, using similes and hyperbole to bring us face-to-face with our reality and the reality of God's love, law and kingdom.

His stories are easy to follow. They often catch the listener by surprise and always make sense on the surface. The difficulty in understanding them comes from the realisation that Jesus is talking about the nature of God, or the kingdom, or discipleship, or even ourselves! Sometimes we too, even with our 21st-century understanding of story and life, can miss the point, because it is too shocking or doesn't fit with our preconceived understandings.

The real challenge when engaging with the parables of Jesus is to dig deeply enough, with an open mind, to try to hear the truth that they contain, and then allow that to impact our understanding and, more importantly, our life.

When we choose to be disciples and desire to be taught and challenged, then our hearts, minds, eyes and ears are able to understand the truth, and we know that the truth shall set us free.

# 2 The sowed seed – keep on proclaiming!

**Luke 8:1–15**

This parable is so well known and so much has been written and taught about it. It was recorded and retold by Mark (4:3–20), Matthew (13:1–23) and Luke, and there are glimpses of it in John's prologue (1:11–13).

There are two main challenges here for us. The first is to trust in the message that we proclaim and to proclaim it. When we recognise that we are called to evangelise, we must trust that the good news we are invited to share is Jesus himself. It is not a set of dogmas based on the living practices of people who follow Jesus. Nor is it treatises or reflections about Jesus. It is Jesus himself. He is the Word. He is the seed. How do we sow this Word?

We sow the Word by being Christ-like. We love and serve; we recognise and affirm the inherent value in all people; and in relationship we discover together that it is Christ in us that leads us on. Look at the stirring words of Dr S.M. Lockridge: 'I wonder; do you know him?' We can trust that Jesus really is the answer, even when we are unsure what the questions really are.

The second challenge is that our role is to proclaim, to sow the seed and to allow God to be God and humanity to be humanity. God's gift to us is our freedom, and we must allow people to reject the 'truth' we proclaim. We cannot compel people to believe; it simply is not God's way and it would go against his gift of free will. When Mark, Luke and Matthew recount this parable, they are speaking to a group of people struggling to come to terms with how to respond to their Jewish brothers and sisters who have rejected Christ. They are coming to terms with the reality that God's message is for all peoples of the world. They are coming to terms with having the 'gift that brings life' and not being able to make their loved ones accept it. These are similar issues that face us: how are we to sow these seeds; what do we do when people we love turn away from what we know will bring them life? The answer, shown in Acts 28:23–31, was understood by Paul. He keeps on proclaiming. The rest, he knows, is up to God.

# 3 Is the prodigal son really sorry?

**Luke 15:11–32**

In telling the parable of the prodigal son, Jesus doesn't say whether or not the son is sorry for his actions. The son simply says that he realises his life would be better at home. He does not express any remorse, but does have an understanding of the nature of his broken relationship with his father.

When he asks for his inheritance, a totally scandalous request, he is to all intents and purposes saying to his father, 'I wish you were dead.' The public shame caused by the son showing so little respect for the father would have been devastating.

The scandal of the story would have been enormous to the people listening. What will happen to the lad? He deserves nothing; no mercy, no grace. In fact, if anybody in the village saw him, he would be chased away, lest more disgrace is heaped on the father.

So he returns with his prepared and practised line, and enough humility perhaps to get some food and a place to stay. Has he learned to love his father through his experience? No, of course not.

The crux of the story lies in the unfathomable grace and mercy of the father. He runs to his son before any words are spoken, restoring the covenant and effectively saying: 'You are still my son; I am still your father.'

So does the son say sorry? Perhaps, during the meal, or maybe in the weeks and months to follow. The profound truth in this parable is that God forgives us *before* we say sorry. His mercy is *not* conditional on an apology, or even an acceptance of our own failures. His mercy is unconditional and we simply have to be in enough of a relationship with him to receive it.

The shepherd goes looking for the lost sheep; the woman searches for the lost coin; when Jesus was dying on the cross, he pleaded with the Father to forgive us, when nobody was sorry.

It seems counterintuitive, but it makes the most sense of God's grace, mercy and sacrifice. We must be careful not to play the older brother here, demanding that the Father recognises our sacrifice, demanding justice on our terms, thinking that somehow we have earned the love that we desire. It was always a gift and our most appropriate response is simply gratitude.

# 4  Sheep and goats, faith and works

**Matthew 25:31–46**

When reflecting on this passage, it is vital to clearly state that we are saved through faith and not works, but also that works are a sign of our saving faith. The distinction is important but also gently nuanced.

Our works often lead us into a deeper appreciation of the saving grace shown to us. It is often when we engage with the neediest people that our faith grows. We recognise our need to rely on God's grace, accepting that we cannot 'sort it out' but must trust in the one who can. Our works often lead us to the Saviour, just as our faith leads us to service.

We can deduce from the writing in the letter of James, in chapter 2, that there was a lively debate in the early church about faith and works. The author of James is very clear that works have a role to play in our salvation; however, Paul's insistence on our justification by faith (Romans 3) is vital in interpreting James' words.

We might consider that we are justified through faith and become righteous through our works. The challenge of today's parable is to recognise that our response to God's love is how our faith is ultimately judged. It gives us the language to make sense of faith. What does it practically look like to say we believe in the saving grace and action of Jesus? Belief must look like service and sacrifice.

When the followers of Jesus in the early church were reminded of Jesus' words by Matthew's Gospel, would they have responded in fear like so many people reading the words today? I suggest that they wouldn't, but they would have taken a moment to consider what their faith looked like in practice. For many people today, the words of this parable strike fear into their hearts because they worry they are not doing enough. If it is a godly fear, then that's OK as it motivates us to give more of ourselves. But if the fear is based on a misconception of who God is, then it's not healthy. Pope Francis has reminded us (in *Misericordiae Vultus*) that God's very nature is mercy. The parable reminds and encourages us that, as we grow in our faith and acceptance of Jesus as our Saviour, we become the sheep, faithfully following the instruction of the shepherd.

# 5 The problem with not producing fruit

Luke 13:6–9

This parable is often looked at as a challenge to and a condemnation of the people of Israel. Many commentators link it to the destruction of Jerusalem by the Romans. They say that is the fulfilment of the story. The implication here is that the Jewish people had their chance: they had three years of the Messiah in their midst, plus an extra 'year' (v. 8) to reflect on the life of the early church, but they still didn't change and so God cut them down. This, I believe, is a harsh interpretation of the parable and probably owes more to anti-Semitism than to good biblical scholarship.

The parable doesn't end. The tree is not cut down. Who knows what intervention the gardener will make after the extra year? And who knows what fruit will grow? After all, the disciples and apostles of the early church were all Jewish, were they not? Surely they must count as fruit of the tree of the nation of Israel. Maybe another way to look at it is to consider Jesus as being the gardener – not an uncommon theme or description; Mary mistakes Jesus for the gardener in John's account of the resurrection (20:14–17). Here, surely, John is playing with the description and linking Jesus back to Eden and creation.

If Jesus is the gardener in the parable, then it becomes a parable of mercy. The gardener recognises that the tree needs to be fed and so sets about intervening on its behalf.

I hesitate to consider the meaning of the manure, but perhaps it has something to do with our own sufferings and how, through these, we allow God's spirit to grow inside us.

We must at some point produce fruit; it is the result of our faith and, as explored in the parable of the sheep and the goats, the sign of our belief. We can, however, trust in the mercy of the one who planted us, and the skill of the gardener helping us to grow and develop. Judgement will come; Jesus will return; some will be chopped down; but we must not be afraid: we have a gardener willing to get his hands dirty by caring for us and nurturing us to life.

# 6 'Go and do likewise': the good Samaritan

**Luke 10:25–37**

One of the beautiful points in this much-loved parable is that the lawyer, who asks Jesus the questions prompting its telling, answers Jesus' questions correctly. Firstly, he recites the law, recognising that this will bring life. Secondly, he highlights the 'one who showed him mercy' (v. 37), recognising this as the fulfilment of the law. The challenge to the lawyer is to really listen and produce fruit.

There is nothing new in Jesus' story; he simply brings the practice of the law to life and shows how we can so often listen to the words but not hear it in our hearts. We listen but do not bear fruit.

The priest and the Levite in the parable are two examples of what it looks like when our focus is on the outward. They get caught up in the lie that their ministry is so important that nothing can get in its way: they must be clean in order to serve the people; they serve the people so that they might be saved. These are the characters that hear the parables but don't understand them. These are the ones on stony or weed-ridden ground. These are the ones whose hearts are hardened and who are blinded by their ideas of who God is.

The lawyer hears the words, understands the teaching and has its seed planted in his soil. We are left wondering, though, what the quality of that soil is.

It may be that once again Jesus is a character in the parable. It may be that he is the good Samaritan, despised by the ones he has come to save. Certainly many writers have considered this, just as many have considered the story as simply about doing good.

The parable is best read as another example of fruitfulness and a challenge to really listen to and hear the word of God in our lives and our hearts. It's never too late to turn back to God, to repent and throw ourselves on his mercy. We have all played the part of the priest or Levite at times and walked on by, but these errors will not be held against us if we trust in God's mercy. 'Let anyone with ears listen!' (Matthew 13:43).

## Guidelines

- Do I really listen to the words of the parables? Do they challenge me anew?
- How fruitful is my faith?
- How much do I believe and trust in the mercy of God?
- What aspect of my life do I need to turn around and receive God's mercy in?
- Am I afraid of God's final judgement on my life?

# Passover psalms

Two out of the four Gospels, in their narration of our Lord's Passion, report that he and his disciples sang as they left the upper room and then journeyed to the Mount of Olives.

Mark, in his account (probably the earliest), records that 'when they had sung the hymn, they went out to the Mount of Olives' (14:26). But what is sung is not specified either by Mark or in Matthew's parallel account (26:30).

Historians and commentators concur with considerable certainty that what was sung was a group of psalms known as the Egyptian Hallel. These comprise Psalms 113—118 (as numbered in Protestant Bibles). The Egyptian Hallel (not to be confused with the Great Hallel consisting of Psalms 120—136) was sung at major Jewish festivals and always at Passover. The dating of individual psalms within this group is no easy issue, but it is most likely they all originate from the post-exilic period. And as a liturgical grouping they were certainly established in use at Jewish festival worship before the time of Christ.

*Hallel* is the Hebrew command to 'Praise the Lord!' found dotted throughout these psalms. And it is called the *Egyptian* Hallel because of the grouping's close association with Passover and the flight of the Israelites from slavery in Egypt. This cycle of psalms would have been chanted antiphonally by priests and people standing before the altar as the Passover lambs were presented for sacrifice.

With the last supper, as in other typical Jewish domestic gatherings, the first two psalms would have been sung before the meal and the remaining four at its end.

There are quotes from the Egyptian Hallel at several points in the New Testament; we shall note these as they occur. Most closely associated with Holy Week, however, is the shout of praise from Psalm 118 taken up by the crowds on Palm Sunday: 'Hosanna... Blessed is the one who comes in the name of the Lord' (Matthew 21:9).

As we reflect on these psalms, as well as considering their original context and meaning, we will ask what it may have meant to Jesus to recite these words at the last supper, as he prayed in Gethsemane, as he was betrayed and deserted, and as he approached his death on the cross. In this way, we can enter into the significance of Holy Week from a fresh perspective.

Quotations are from the New Revised Standard Version.

# 1 A god like our God?

**Psalm 113**

This psalm of praise is in two parts. Verses 1–4 issue a call to worship and, in quite an exceptional manner, declare the greatness of God's name and the matchlessness of his glory. The remainder (vv. 5–9) invites us to ponder God's activity on behalf of the poor and needy, and to ask whether there is any god like our God.

The reach of God's control and power is asserted. He is worthy of praise at all times and in all places. Yet the Sovereign Lord who reigns on high stoops to be with and to raise up the vulnerable and destitute. Jesus, God's incarnate Son, has come among us as the concrete expression of God's limitless love and saving action. Verses 7–8 find an echo in Mary's Magnificat (Luke 1, especially vv. 52–53).

One example of the needy specified in this psalm is the childless woman. The Hebrew reveals a play on words: the Lord who makes his own dwelling in the heavens (v. 4) is the one who makes a dwelling for the barren woman (v. 9).

Biblically, we think of Sarah, Elizabeth and especially Hannah (vv. 7–8 are almost identical to 1 Samuel 2:8). We think of several women – most likely childless – that were drawn to Jesus. Examples include the woman bent double (Luke 13:10–17) and the woman with a flow of blood (Luke 8:43–48 and parallels); the widow of Nain, faced with the loss of her son, is another (Luke 7:11–16).

But what of Jesus' mother who would soon lose her firstborn? In his death, Jesus makes provision for her: she is tenderly entrusted to the care of John the disciple (John 19:26–27).

And what of Jesus himself? He would not be spared. God would not answer his cry for deliverance in Gethsemane or his cry of dereliction from the cross. But it is because he lies in the dust and sits on the ash heap that we are raised to newness of life. Verse 8 proclaims a great reversal: the poor and needy will sit with princes. Jesus is now seated at the right hand of God on high – and one day we who are made from the dust of the earth will be seated with him. Is there any god like our God? Indeed, there is not!

# 2 Looking back... looking up...

In this grouping of psalms for Passover, only Psalm 114 explicitly mentions the Exodus. With great power and subtlety, initial joy gives way to reverent awe. Notice how creation is personified: the sea flees, Jordan retreats, the mountains gambol. All bow to God's command, but all also rejoice at his saving work.

The Exodus was the single greatest display of God's redemptive power during the Old Testament era, but unusually this psalm focuses more on the events that follow: God's compassionate provision in the wilderness (compare Numbers 20) and the crossing of the Jordan into the promised land.

During these years of pilgrimage, not only is God Israel's refuge and sanctuary, the rock of safety to whom they flee in times of trouble, but Israel is also God's sanctuary, the people among whom he makes his dwelling. The tabernacle, and later the temple, would be the place where he dwelt and could be approached.

The psalmist asks why creation behaves in the way it does: why does the sea flee and the Jordan retreat; why do the mountains skip and the hills gambol like lambs?

The answer comes in the final two verses. Just as the people of Israel once did when Sinai shook and God revealed himself in the giving of the law, the whole of creation and all humanity must tremble at the presence of almighty God. God comes to judge, to sweep away the old, enslaving order (compare Revelation 20:11), and to usher in a new creation.

God's judgement is the corollary of his redeeming work. This psalm is framed with references to Jacob, the name given to unredeemed Israel. God transforms the least promising into something new and truly glorious. The Hebrew rendered 'tremble' in verse 7 can mean to tremble either with fear or with wonder. The New English Bible translates it as, 'Dance, O earth.'

At his transfiguration, Jesus, we are told, discussed with Moses and Elijah his forthcoming 'departure' (Luke 9:31). The Greek word here is *exodus*.

Just a few hours after singing this psalm at the last supper, Jesus' life would be swept away as the judgement that should have been ours flooded over him. But on the third day, the waters of death would turn back and flee at God's command, and a new creation would come into view. At this all the earth should surely tremble with the highest joy and deepest reverence.

# 3  Where is our God?

**Psalm 115**

A concern for God's name runs throughout scripture. In the ten commandments, the Lord's name is not to be taken in vain but honoured. And in the Lord's Prayer, it is to be 'hallowed', that is, revered and respected as holy.

Psalm 115 (in the Greek version, it is a continuation of the preceding psalm) focuses on dealing with the threat implied in verse 2: why should other nations say of the Jews, 'Where is their God?' A failure of God to bless – with crops, with children or against Israel's enemies, for example – could be taken as signifying that the Lord God of Israel was no better, and perhaps weaker, than the gods worshipped by surrounding enemy nations.

It is likely that this psalm has the exile as its backdrop. The colourful invective against foreign gods is highly reminiscent of the latter part of Isaiah (note especially 44:9–20; 46:6–13). These prophetic words would have been a great encouragement to the Jews living under foreign rule in Babylon.

The remainder of the psalm, from verse 9 onwards, is a blend of prayer and promise. There is both request for God's blessing and prophetic assurance that this blessing will come. The assurance rests not on anything God's people can bring about, but in the knowledge that God is a jealous God and will not allow his name to lie in the dust or the praise of his people to fall silent (v. 17). God's will – and it is fundamental to his will that he receives unending praise – shall be done on earth just as it is done in heaven (v. 16).

In Gethsemane, Jesus prayed, 'Not my will, but yours be done' (Luke 22:42). He 'entrusted himself to the one who judges justly' (1 Peter 2:23). And at the moment of death, he commended his spirit to God's keeping (Luke 23:46). At the heart of Psalm 115 is the command to 'trust in the Lord'. It comes three times in as many verses (vv. 9–11). And three times we are assured that he is our 'help' and 'shield'.

We are invited to contemplate Jesus' perfect trust and obedience, and to consider how deeply our faith runs.

# 4  A song of thanksgiving

Of the psalms in this collection, it is not hard to imagine Psalm 116 forming the core of the prayers Jesus offered in Gethsemane and subsequently, as he shouldered the weight of the crossbeam through the narrow streets of Jerusalem.

The writer sings of his deliverance as though it is a past event: 'He has heard my voice' (v. 1). But it is evident he remains in imminent mortal danger. He confidently anticipates a future deliverance, a time when he will once more lift up the cup of salvation and make his vows of thanksgiving and consecration to the Lord.

The exact nature of the threat is unclear – illness, injury or personal weakness, perhaps – but there are also treacherous third parties present (vv. 10–11). The Gospels reveal the interlocked threats faced by Jesus: not only the pain and shame of crucifixion, but also the injustice of his trial, betrayal by one of his own disciples and the desertion of friends.

The writer uses multiple expressions to declare his innocence and commitment: he has acted with integrity and simplicity (vv. 6, 9), he has kept the faith (v. 10), and he is a humble servant of the Lord (v. 16).

The New Testament suggests that a central factor in Jesus' ability to remain faithful even unto death was that he held in view what lay beyond and 'for the sake of the joy that was set before him endured the cross' (Hebrews 12:2).

At the last supper Jesus lifts the cup of salvation, a covenant vow that, for the sake of his disciples, he will fulfil his God-given mission. And as he lifts it, he knows he will not drink it again until he enters his Father's kingdom (Mark 14:25), having by his death and resurrection put beyond doubt the greatness and graciousness of God.

The apostle Paul likewise speaks of having finished the race, having kept the faith (2 Timothy 4:7; compare Psalm 116:10). Hope, resting on the past fulfilment of God's promises, is faith looking to the future. Paul, obliquely citing Psalm 116, declares, 'This slight momentary affliction is preparing us for an eternal weight of glory... because we look not at what can be seen, but at what cannot be seen; for what can be seen is temporary, but what cannot be seen is eternal' (2 Corinthians 4:13, 17–18).

# 5 A simple creed and a clear call

Psalm 117

Sandwiched between two much longer songs, Psalm 117 is the briefest in the Psalter and the shortest chapter in scripture. Yet this potent little psalm reaches both backwards and forwards to give a succinct summary of the sweep and scope of salvation.

If Psalm 116 focuses our attention on the last supper, Psalm 117 vibrates with the joy of Pentecost and the subsequent worldwide spread of the gospel. All nations and all peoples are to praise the Lord. The reason? Simple! His steadfast love is great and his faithfulness eternal.

This psalm can be taken to support a doctrine of universalism, the notion that all will eventually be embraced by God's saving plan and none excluded. This is not the interpretation of the apostle Paul who quotes this psalm – among others – in Romans 15 (v. 11). Paul takes us back to God's covenant promise to Abraham, the declaration that, through him and his descendants, God's blessings will be made available to all families on earth (Genesis 12:1–4).

Israel was never intended to keep God's blessings for herself: the nation was to be a light to the Gentiles. And for Paul, Jesus the Jewish Messiah is the sole means of salvation for the whole earth. Hence the imperative to make the gospel known, and the call to all nations to honour the one Lord, now revealed in Christ.

Jesus was angry on occasion at the exclusiveness of the Jewish authorities. The temple, he argued vehemently and with violence, should be a house of prayer for all nations (Mark 11:17). And he anticipated that after Pentecost, filled with the joy of the resurrection and the empowering presence of the Spirit, his followers would take the good news to every corner of the earth (Acts 1:8). Paul, the apostle to the Gentiles, saw himself as pioneering and participating in that process, the mission that today still remains the principal uncompleted task of the church.

The psalmist's confidence rests in the knowledge that God's love will prevail – a vigorous word used of the stronger side in battle, and a better rendering of the word 'great' in verse 2. The book of Revelation envisages the completion of the process: 'There was a great multitude that no one could count, from every nation, from all tribes and people and languages, standing before the throne and before the Lamb' (Revelation 7:9).

# 6 Hosanna in the highest

**Psalm 118**

This, the last and longest of the psalms that form the Egyptian Hallel, is an obvious song of triumph. While Psalm 116 reflects the heat of battle but anticipates a final victory, Psalm 118 largely looks back on a victory that's been secured, but nevertheless contains suggestions that the battle may not be entirely over and there are other skirmishes still to fight (see, for example, vv. 6, 7 and 25).

There are several quotations from this psalm in the New Testament. Jesus claimed to be the stone that the builders rejected but that was chosen by God as the all-important load-bearing cornerstone (Luke 20:17; compare Acts 4:11 and 1 Peter 2:7). The metaphor originates in Isaiah 28:16.

Better known, however, is the psalm's use on Palm Sunday: all four Gospels record its adoption by the crowds that greet Jesus' arrival in Jerusalem. The call 'Lord, save us' (v. 25) becomes the shout of 'Hosanna!' and explains the latter's essential meaning. They continue with praise: 'Blessed is he who comes in the name of the Lord!' (Matthew 21:9; Mark 11:9; John 12:13).

The victory in view in the psalm is the overpowering of foreign nations despite their apparently superior strength. We might see parts of this psalm as rather crude expressions of triumph: for instance, the refrain in verses 10–12: 'In the name of the Lord I cut them down' (NIV). But that is to judge this psalm by our more modern, but not necessarily more enlightened, code of ethics.

In fact, there is little in this psalm that is self-congratulatory or jingoistic: the writer's victory is throughout ascribed to the steadfast love of the Lord, a covenantal love in which we can put our utter confidence. The writer's determination is to share the joy of this victory with others who are like-minded, and together to process to the temple of the Lord to bring him appropriate and heartfelt thanksgiving.

'Was it not necessary that the Messiah should suffer these things and then enter his glory?' (Luke 24:26). Christ shares the rewards of his triumph with us; and we offer him our shouts of praise and acclamations of thanksgiving.

# Guidelines

It is of course impossible to know fully or even partially what was in the mind of the Lord as he approached each stage of his Passion. We do know he agonised over what lay ahead and wrestled with God in prayer as he submitted to what he discerned as God's will for him. Can we doubt that he saw himself as the instrument of God's saving plan as revealed in scripture? Can we doubt that Jesus took strength and guidance from scripture? And can we doubt that he used the words of scripture, perhaps especially these psalms, as his vehicle for prayer?

The psalms of the Egyptian Hallel had a particular resonance and meaning for the Jewish people of Jesus' time as they, an occupied nation, marked Passover year by year. Can we doubt that the same psalms, sung by Jesus and his disciples on the night of his betrayal – thus setting in motion his arrest, trial, torture and journey through Jerusalem to Golgotha – in some deep way spoke to Jesus and sustained him, the one who is for us our Passover lamb?

Looking back, are there any scriptures that have sustained or guided you in times of challenge or change in your life? Think of three or four key life events: were there particular passages that enabled you to discover God's purposes in what you were experiencing?

And what of the present and future? Is there one of these six psalms from which you could take strength or that you could make your vehicle of prayer as you continue your pilgrim journey?

**FURTHER READING**

Geoffrey W. Grogan, *Psalms (Two Horizons Old Testament Commentary)* (Eerdmans, 2008).

W.J. Harrelson (ed.), *The New Interpreter's Study Bible* (Abingdon Press, 2003).

Derek Kidner, *Psalms 72–150 (Tyndale Old Testament Commentary Series)* (IVP, 1975).

# Praying our sorrows

When people describe the Psalms, most identify themes of praise and thanksgiving. Of course the Psalter contains many psalms that stress these two expressions of faith, but there is a third. Lament psalms provide another significant and, I would argue, equally important expression. Around one-third of the psalms in the Psalter are clearly laments, which leads James Crenshaw to say that these psalms are the 'backbone' of the Psalter!

Lament psalms typically express a person's, or a community's, response to a distressing experience. Scholars have identified these psalms in different ways. Claus Westermann, in *Praise and Lament in the Psalms*, calls them laments. For him, lament psalms offer a pathway for expressing distress. He also notes that as we read through the Psalter from beginning to end, lament psalms decrease in number while praise and thanksgiving psalms increase in number. Westermann suggests that the decreasing number of laments as the Psalter unfolds is a picture of a growing life of faith.

Erhard Gerstenberger calls them psalms of complaint. Of course, the complaint is always accompanied by a plea or petition asking God to respond. While these and other perspectives are helpful, I view these psalms as psalms of distress. Their primary focus is identifying distress, describing responses to distress and imagining hope beyond the distress. Such a process of engagement and expression of a desire for help leads to a place of hope. It is this dynamic that we will explore over the following six reflections.

Each lament psalm offers a beginning point to experience the intrinsic power of lament. When they are used alongside praise and thanksgiving, they form a powerful triad of prayer. It might be helpful to imagine prayer in the Psalter as balanced on these three 'legs' like a stool. If any one of praise, thanksgiving or lament is missing or under-represented, then the prayer life of the believer can lose a sense of equilibrium and become unbalanced.

Quotations are from the New Revised Standard Version.

# 1 A reality check

Psalm 3 follows two psalms that reinforce the idea of blessing for those who live a righteous life and God's sovereignty. On first glance it may seem out of place. If Psalms 1 and 2 hold true, then why lament? Abruptly, this psalm directs us to the reality of lived experience for all human beings. It recognises that distress is a reality, even for those seeking to live a right life and believing that God is sovereign. As a reflection of lived experience, it is a most valuable challenge to the simplistic view that suggests a person of faith ought never to be distressed and has nothing to complain about.

The title of Psalm 3 identifies this as a prayer of David. Here is the one who was 'after God's own heart' desperately calling out to God in his distress. Even though David desires to live a righteous life and presumably believes that God is sovereign, he still expresses his distress. It seems that, from a human perspective, the rewards of a righteous life and belief in God's sovereignty are not always so clear. This is the realm of lament. As you read through this psalm, there are a few features that are worth noting. Firstly, the psalmist quotes the words of the enemy, reminding God of what has been said: 'There is no help for you in God' (v. 2). Despite this, however, the psalmist then quickly asserts in verse 3 that there is yet hope in God who protects ('a shield around me'/'lifts up my head'). This is followed by a plea for help and another feature of these psalms that troubles some: technically referred to as imprecation, psalmists sometimes express violence towards their enemies. Imprecations are typically expressed in direct language but the desired action is consigned to God. Perhaps this reminds us that those who distress us often bring out the worst in us. Here the psalmist expresses violent feelings unashamedly, but understands that any violent action is something only God ought to use.

Because of what is expressed in the body of this psalm, the ending may seem a little surprising. However, in some ways it echoes the sentiments of Psalms 1 and 2. The psalmist, trusting in God, will eventually see divine deliverance from distress, and blessing will rest on God's people. Those seeking to live the way of the righteous will trust in God's sovereignty.

# 2 Questioning God

The two psalms preceding Psalm 10 reinforce similar concepts to Psalms 1 and 2. As a result, Psalm 10 jolts us like Psalm 3. It brings us back to earth, reminding us that sometimes God does seem distant, especially when we feel distressed. As is often the case, the lamenting psalmist begins with questions. They are rhetorical, expressing the psalmist's sense of alienation from God and fears in their situation.

Following the initial questions, the psalmist then gives a detailed description of those causing the distress (vv. 2–11). Despite the detail, we have no idea who or what the enemy is. Sometimes the enemy is real, and sometimes metaphorical. In Psalm 10 the enemy is made up of many – all those who are wicked and prosper. In contrast, the psalmist is not prospering. This kind of prayer offers a direct challenge and even critique of the theology found in Psalm 1. It suggests that the picture painted in Psalm 1 might be an ideal, but the lived reality of people of faith can vary from this ideal – at times, dramatically!

All is not lost, though, because the psalmist then asks for divine intervention. 'Rise up, O Lord; O God, lift up your hand' (v. 12) is a strong assertion that God can do something about the psalmist's distress. It marks a rise in confidence that may seem surprising. How could a distressed person, feeling distanced from God, call out as confidently as this? Perhaps because the Psalter reminds us, through psalms of praise and thanksgiving, that while God may at times seem distant or absent, or may even seem to be powerless, this is not reality. These psalms have a wonderful way of asserting God's capacity to act in response to distress. Verses 15 and 16 assert God's power dramatically, again echoing Psalm 2.

By praying in this way, the psalmist trusts in God's action and deliverance even before it happens. Even though Psalm 10 opens with a deep sense of despair, it ends with a hopeful imagined future. The psalm culminates in a resounding sense of hope amid distress. The hopeful vision at the end of Psalm 10 does not suggest that praying like this inevitably removes distress. It does, however, offer a way of expressing distress to God through prayer. Providing such permission can become a catalyst for hope.

# 3 Reminding God

This psalm expands the questioning we encountered in Psalm 10 with a series of five heart-wrenching expressions. It seems as though the psalmist feels that God is an enemy as well. The second question, 'Will you forget me forever?' voices the anguish caused by God's seeming lack of concern for the person in distress. Distress is found in every direction. But again, these feelings of despair are formed into a prayer to God – even though he may be an enemy!

The questions form a bridge to a plea for help. It is a strong request by the psalmist which almost seems to be demanding: 'Consider and answer me, O Lord my God' (v. 3). It seems as though the psalmist even uses leverage with God to get a response by appealing to God's honour. If God does not respond then the enemy can say, 'I have prevailed' (v. 4). Perhaps as a way of reinforcing this leverage, there is also an appeal to God's 'steadfast love' in verse 5. This is the Hebrew word *chesed*, which is a covenantal term. The psalmist is implicitly asking God to remember the covenant with its inherent promises of protection. This is particularly relevant in a situation of distress.

The appeal to the covenant also marks a subtle but important shift. While God is accused of forgetting in verse 1, the appeal to *chesed* is a call for God to remember. In remembering the covenant, God will remember the psalmist in distress. When God remembers the covenant, God acts. We see an example of this in Exodus 2:24–25, where 'God heard their groaning, and remembered his covenant with Abraham, Isaac and Jacob. God looked on the Israelites, and God took notice of them.' It is reasonable to imagine that this is what the psalmist is appealing to in the prayer of Psalm 13.

As Psalm 10 ended with an imagined future of praise to God, so Psalm 13 ends similarly. However, in this case it is not universalised like it was in Psalm 10. Here, the rejoicing and singing is a personal expression of thanks to God for deliverance from distress. In ancient Israel, thanks would have been offered in the congregation. Viewing the end of these two laments together (Psalms 10 and 13) reminds us that God's deliverance has both personal and universal implications. It also underlines that, even in the midst of deep despair, there is reason to be confident in divine deliverance from distress.

# 4  The cry of abandonment

**Psalm 22**

Psalm 22 is possibly best known for its opening question, voiced by Christ on the cross. However, long before the life and times of Christ, this psalm was included in the Psalter and used in the liturgy of the second temple. The fact that Jesus used Psalm 22 on the cross simply reinforces the value of these kinds of psalms. It just so happens that, in this case, Jesus recited at least the opening lines of this psalm at a profound juncture in human history. So how much does the psalm contribute to our understanding of distress expressed as prayer?

You might notice as you read through the psalm that it seems rather disjointed. It begins with a series of questions, like Psalm 13. Abruptly though, it then shifts to a series of assertions in verses 3–5, which form the basis of a plea for God's help much later in the psalm. The middle section of the psalm is a personal reflection that expresses both the frailty of humanity and our dependence on God. As with the other psalms we have considered, here is a person in distress who recognises the depth of their distress but who is also aware that God hears the cry of the weak.

Verses 12–18 present a protracted description of the psalmist's complaint, using the powerful imagery of strong bulls, bones out of joint, melting wax and others. These images produce a potent collage and also evoke emotions in the reader. Again, this psalm contains a jolting shift, here found in verse 19. Following the expression of emotion and assertions about God, the psalmist now presents a clear plea for help. This expands broadly into a commitment to praise and recognition that God's purposes on the earth are universal. Somehow, out of expressing despair, hope begins to emerge for the future. Imagination is enhanced and the psalmist can both pray and hope amid distress.

Much could be added about the reason this psalm figures in the crucifixion. Briefly, it's worth reflecting on the closing images as much as the opening questions to appreciate its relevance. While the psalm is deeply and intensely personal, it also highlights the broader purposes of God's work in the world. While the cry of Christ on the cross was one of abandonment, the close of the psalm reminds us that this is not the end of the story. Redemption is at hand, in the fullest sense of the word.

# 5 When the community laments

The previous four laments we have considered are all from an individual. In contrast, Psalm 44 reflects a community in distress. Psalms like this remind us that communities lament as well as individuals. Psalm 44 also begins in a different way from what we have observed so far. At first glance, it doesn't even appear to be a lament psalm. The first eight verses of the prayer paint God as the champion who has secured victory for the people, seemingly without exception. There appears to be complete trust in God's action against those who had sought to afflict the people, causing distress or even seeking their destruction.

As we have observed previously though, lament psalms can shift dramatically. In Psalm 44 this occurs in a most jarring way. We encounter a bold accusation in verse 9: 'Yet you have rejected us and abased us.' At the core of the community's distress is the fact that God has acted on their behalf in the past but is not doing so now. But God is not perceived to be inactive. God is the one who has 'abased' them. The following five verses (vv. 10–14) expand on this, all beginning with the second person pronoun 'You'.

This accusatory language is too confrontational for many Christians. It is felt by some that distress ought to be humbly and demurely accepted. While most would not deny the privilege we have as people of faith in asking God for help, it seems that the strong language of Psalm 44 is, perhaps, too extreme for some. Whatever our view, though, the words are here, recorded as the prayer of a faith community in distress. There is no attempt to diminish the distress or the frustration and anger with God who seems, at best, powerless and, at worst, to be causing or aggravating the distress.

Of course, the psalm doesn't end with this sentiment. The middle section (vv. 17–22) contains a strong assertion of the community's faithfulness. Their faithfulness is pitched in direct contrast to how God seems to be acting. However, despite or perhaps because of these thoughts and feelings being voiced, a hopeful imagining again emerges at the close of the psalm. The use of covenant terms such as 'redeem' and 'steadfast love' remind us that confidence in God, amid distress, can still be found in the covenant relationship God has with people. Distress is always distressing but can also be reimagined as redemptive suffering.

# 6  When there seems to be no hope

This psalm is unique in the Psalter. Although clearly a lament, a significant element is absent: there is no sense of the imagined future present in other lament psalms. We will return to this lack of hope later in our reflection. The psalmist could be facing death, reflected in expressions such as, 'my life draws near to Sheol' (v. 3). It is clear that the situation is dire. No matter how dire though, the distress is expressed to God. The psalmist begins with a sense of confidence by calling on the 'Lord, God of my salvation' (v. 1). Perhaps this is an implicit plea for mercy by the psalmist. Ironically, as previously observed, God can be viewed as the enemy at times and this sentiment is also found here in verses 6–7. The tone here is strongly accusatory.

Unlike the community in Psalm 44, the psalmist here does not assert any sense of innocence. Rather than using a presumed innocence and faithfulness as the reason for God to help, the psalmist simply appeals to God's mercy. The psalm contains a series of expressions to this effect, such as: 'let my prayer come before you' (v. 2), 'Every day I call on you, O Lord' (v. 9) and 'But I, O Lord, cry out to you' (v. 13). It is obvious that the cry for mercy is directed solely to God.

We now return to the uniqueness of this lament psalm mentioned above. The absence of an imagined future is obvious when contrasted with the other psalms we have considered. One might expect that this psalm, like others, would end on a high note of hope. Failing this, perhaps hope may be found somewhere else in the psalm. Not here, though. This absence of hope might seem deeply disturbing, especially for Christians. However, the psalm holds an important message. It reminds us that there are situations in life that cannot have any hope, at least in our lived experience this side of death – for example, when someone we deeply love dies or when we are diagnosed with an incurable illness. Even for a person of faith, these distresses thrust us into a similar position to that of the psalmist in Psalm 88. All that can be done is to throw ourselves on the mercy of God. The psalm is an expression of trust that God is the one who saves and it is with God that our life and death finally rests.

# Guidelines

Exploring some selected lament psalms this week leads to some important points for reflection and action. The following questions will help to focus your thoughts about these kinds of psalms:

- Which emotions associated with distress do you detect being expressed in the lament psalms we have considered?
- What kinds of things do the psalmists assert about themselves, their community and God?
- In what ways do the psalmists 'invest' or express trust in God through their lament prayers?
- Is it realistic to think that hope for the future could be imagined as we pray these psalms, reflecting on distress in our lives?
- How do you react to the imprecations in some lament psalms (calling on God to inflict violence on 'enemies')? Do you think this has a place for Christians responding to their distress?

As an activity, you might like to try writing a lament psalm of your own. Use the simple framework suggested below as a starting point:

- Begin by expressing the emotions associated with your distress. This may be in the form of questions such as those contained in many lament psalms.
- Then assert yourself with a clearly articulated plea for God to respond to your distress. Part of this might be stating what you think God is able to do and what you might be able to do in the face of your distress.
- You might like to include some thoughts as to why you invest in God as one who can be trusted when you are in distress.
- Finally, write about what a hopeful future might look like beyond distress.

Another approach is to paint a picture, create a sculpture or compose some music along these lines instead of using words. You may be able to think of some other ways in which you can creatively express your lament.

**FURTHER READING**

Robert Alter, *The Book of Psalms: Translation with commentary* (W.W. Norton, 2007).

David J. Cohen, *Why O Lord?* (Paternoster Press, 2013).

Erhard Gerstenberger, *Psalms: Part 1 with an introduction to cultic poetry*, vol. 14 (Eerdmans, 1988).

Erhard Gerstenberger, *Psalms, Part 2, and Lamentations* (Eerdmans, 2001).

Roger Van Harn, *Psalms for Preaching and Worship: A lectionary commentary* (Eerdmans, 2009).

Bruce K. Waltke, J. M. Houston and Erika Moore, *The Psalms as Christian Worship: A historical commentary* (Eerdmans, 2010).

Claus Westermann, Keith R. Crim and Richard N. Soulen, *Praise and Lament in the Psalms* (J. Knox Press, 1981).

# Resurrection in the epistles

When I came to faith as a teenager, I was taught that I could know the forgiveness and love of God because of Jesus' death on the cross for my sins – and that this made all the difference. It did indeed, and the sense of security I found from encountering divine love gradually seeped into and transformed every section of my life. But I remember very clearly one day, as I was walking to church, thinking, 'If Jesus' death achieves everything, why does the resurrection matter?' A common answer is that it was the proof that Jesus was who he said he was, and that his death really does mean forgiveness. Debate then follows about the historical evidence for the resurrection, and whether it is 'objectively true'.

This is important, but it is only one part of Paul's perspective on the resurrection. As we engage with this fascinating exploration, we will find two important correctives to my early understanding. The first is that Paul views the cross and resurrection as two inseparable parts of one great movement of grace, in which God deals with human sin and enmity, and so reconciles humanity to himself. Paul would never have imagined the possibility of talking about the cross without the resurrection. The second is that Paul always sees this one act of cross-and-resurrection as both objective *and* subjective. It is about what God has done for us in Jesus – but it also shapes the whole of Christian life. The physical movement of baptism, down into the water and up again, becomes for Paul the shape of Christian living as our old life 'in the flesh' dies in the death of Jesus, and our new life 'in the Spirit' begins in the resurrection of Jesus. We now begin to live the kingdom life of the age to come, though we do so in the context of this age which is 'passing away'.

This leads to transformation as, free from fear, we are able to give ourselves in love and service just as Jesus did ('losing your life', Matthew 10:39). But it also roots us in hope of life beyond death as we anticipate our own resurrection just as Jesus did. As we read through Paul's letters, we see him opening up each of these issues in turn – and see the difference it makes for Paul, his readers and us today.

Quotations are from the New International Version (Anglicised).

# 1 Jesus' resurrection and ours

**1 Thessalonians 1:9–10; 4:13—5:11**

This is probably Paul's earliest letter, written from Corinth in AD51 or 52, and the verses at the end of chapter 1 offer a fascinating summary of Paul's gospel. Luke summarises Paul's preaching as being centred around Jesus the Messiah, who had to 'suffer and rise from the dead' (Acts 17:3). To accept this involved 'turning' (1 Thessalonians 1:9), a synonym for the repentance invited by Jesus in his preaching, and for Gentiles this meant rejecting their pagan religious past. Paul hints at the importance of Jesus' resurrection – that it was part of God's vindication of who he was, along with his ascension to heaven, and that it is the grounds of our hope – as well as the importance of Jesus' return and of our security when he comes in judgement.

Paul then expands on these themes in chapters 4 and 5. He uses the metaphor of 'sleep' for death (4:13, 15); because of Jesus' resurrection, death has lost its power over us and should no longer be feared. The pattern of God's dealing with Jesus (death followed by resurrection) is the pattern for all who are now in Christ, so we face death with a unique sense of hope. At his return, those who have died will themselves experience resurrection. The language of 'meet the Lord in the air' (4:17) has been widely misunderstood as suggesting that we leave earth to be raptured to heaven before a time of tribulation comes to those left behind. But Paul is clear that he is describing not Christians' departure from earth but Jesus' arrival – his 'coming down from heaven' – and the language he uses (*parousia*, v. 15) draws on the description of a king returning to a city he rules after a long absence. Just as the elders would have come out of the city to greet the king, whose authority they had exercised in his absence, and would have turned to enter the city with him, so we will turn and go with Jesus 'as a kingdom and priests to reign on earth' with him for ever (Revelation 5:10).

This day will come as a 'thief in the night' (1 Thessalonians 5:2) for those unprepared – a metaphor not for its imminence, as though Paul expected Jesus to return in his lifetime, but for its unexpectedness. But we, who are already living resurrection lives, will welcome him instead as a friend in the day.

# 2 Living in the resurrection age

In his other early letter, to Christians in the region of Galatia, Paul mentions resurrection only once, but it underpins his argument in key places. As with 1 Thessalonians 1:9–10, he includes in the opening here a summary of his message. Like other Jews of his time, Paul understands human history to be divided into two ages: the 'present evil age' (1:4) in which sin reigns, God is not acknowledged and his people are oppressed; and the 'age to come' (Ephesians 1:21) in which evil is defeated, the glory of God is revealed and his people worship in freedom.

A key sign of the end of this age and the coming of the next was to be the resurrection of the dead – which is why Jesus' resurrection is always central to Paul's proclamation (see Acts 17:18). When God 'raised him from the dead' it was not merely his vindication – it was also the beginning of the promised new age of God's rule (his kingdom) in which those who are 'in Christ' now live. This age has not yet come to an end, but Jesus' death means that it no longer has power over us – it is no longer our reality – because he has broken the power of sin and death by dying for us and rising again.

Paul is clear that the coming of this new resurrection age means an end to the distinction between those given the law and those outside the covenant people of God. In fact, the law had always been God's gift to his people, and their obedience was a sign of belonging to the covenant, not a means to impress God. Because Jesus, who 'knew no sin, became sin for us' (2 Corinthians 5:21), his death has put to death the power of our sinful human nature, so that we now live the resurrection life of Jesus, made real in us by his Spirit. This is through the faith of Christ which can mean our faith in him – or, perhaps better, his faithfulness to us. We trust him for this resurrection life because his resurrection has shown him to be trustworthy, the supreme victor over death whom we can trust with our very selves.

# 3 The foundation of faith

**1 Corinthians 15:1–19**

We will spend some time in this chapter, because it is the most extended and developed reflection by Paul on the resurrection. Having talked in the preceding chapters about the true nature of spiritual maturity and how that works out in communal life, he now turns to a new subject and offers a concise summary of his gospel, one that corresponds with the concerns of the written Gospels.

Core to Paul's primary belief are three connected things: firstly, that Jesus 'died for our sins' (v. 3); secondly, that God raised him from the dead; and thirdly, that this is what the apostles testify to. Paul doesn't go into details here of what he means by 'died for our sins'; he explores that in greater depth in Romans, but he also summarises it in later correspondence with the Corinthians: our sins have made us enemies with God, but his gracious offer of forgiveness through the sacrifice of Jesus has allowed us to be 'reconciled', transformed from enemies to friends of God (2 Corinthians 5:18–21; compare Ephesians 2:14–16). The fact that Jesus was buried shows that his death was real – he was dead and gone, so resurrection was God's giving of new life, and a new kind of life, transcending death and not mere resuscitation. The nature of apostolic testimony is highlighted by Paul's classing of himself as one 'abnormally born' (v. 8): the usual testimony was based on an apostle's physical encounter with the physically resurrected Jesus, so Paul was unusual in having met Jesus in a vision following his ascension.

There are two threads that run through this threefold tradition. The first is that it all happened 'according to the Scriptures', (vv. 3, 4) which for Paul must have meant fulfilment of the Old Testament – not so much in specific predictions, but in the pattern of God's dealings with his people, as he turns rejection into redemption and brings new life to his people even in the face of death. The second is that this core gospel isn't Paul's personal conviction; he has 'passed on' what he 'received' (v. 3), and it is what we, the whole body of the apostles, preach as a trustworthy testimony to what God has done for us in Christ. This double thread runs through the four Gospels – Jesus' death and resurrection, in fulfilment of the scriptures, is the shared apostolic testimony.

# 4 Personal hope

**1 Corinthians 15:20–41**

Having set out the content of his gospel (in terms of Greek rhetoric, the *logos*), Paul now makes a case for its credibility by overcoming objections (establishing its credibility, or *ethos*). As in 1 Thessalonians 4, he uses the metaphor of sleep for those who have died, and links the destiny of those who have died in the faith of Jesus with Jesus' own destiny. This is expressed by the idea of 'firstfruits' (v. 20): when a farmer sows his crop, one corner of the field will get perhaps a little more rain, or more sun, than the rest, and the crop there will ripen first. Ready for harvest before the main crop, it becomes a sign of what the whole of the field will become in time. Sinful humanity, 'in Adam' (v. 22), can only look forward to experiencing what Adam experienced when he died as a result of turning from God. But redeemed humanity, 'in Christ' (v. 22), can now look forward to experiencing resurrection beyond death just as Jesus did. The reliability of the apostolic testimony to Jesus' resurrection offers the certainty of hope for our own destiny.

Although this hope is for the future, it casts its light back into the contemporary world, transforming life and making a positive difference in the present. 'Those who are baptised for the dead' (v. 29) is an obscure phrase, but it has nothing to do with rituals on behalf of those who have died (as taught by Mormons). It more probably refers to those who have come to faith and been baptised because of the example of friends and family who have faced death with the hope that Jesus' resurrection offers. Such hope transforms Paul's own ministry: he is ready to risk life and limb in obedience to God's call, since he knows that death does not have the final word. And it also transforms our ethical approach to life: if eternity involves living bodily in the presence of God, then our lives in our bodies now have eternal significance, and we should turn from things that will perish and instead invest in what is of lasting value.

Perhaps we cannot imagine what this transformed, bodily life will look like. But that should not worry us – after all, the plant that grows from a seed does not look like the seed, even though it is clearly the same organism. Just as the risen Jesus was both hidden and recognisable, our resurrection bodies will have continuity and discontinuity with the bodily life we now live.

# 5 Cosmic fulfilment

**1 Corinthians 15:42–58**

In the last part of this chapter, Paul moves from the content (*logos*) and credibility (*ethos*) to the emotional and pastoral appeal (*pathos*) of his teaching. He does so by drawing a series of contrasts between life in this age and the resurrection life in the age to come – but it is important to note that his contrast between the 'natural' and the 'spiritual' (vv. 44, 46) or between the 'earthly' and the 'heavenly' (vv. 40, 48, 49) is always between two different kinds of bodies. At no point does Paul follow Greek philosophical ideas that death or resurrection involve the escape of the spirit from the body to join God in heaven.

The reason for the contrast between our present bodies and the bodies we shall be 'clothed with' (p.54) in the resurrection is rooted in the contrast between the first Adam and Jesus, the second 'Adam' – each the progenitor of a kind of humanity. Adam was created to be in the image of God and to live in relationship with God, a destiny destroyed by his disobedience and sin. It is worth noting here that Paul sees Adam and Jesus as kinds of human, not males; English translations add the noun 'man' to verses 48 and 49 where Paul simply has the adjectives 'earthly' and 'heavenly'. Without the redemption that is in Jesus, we live in the image of Adam and experience the same frailty and mortality because of our sin, and so will perish. By contrast Jesus, the image of the invisible God (Colossians 1:15), was obedient to the point of death (Philippians 2:8), thereby defeating the power of both sin and death. When we are 'in Christ', bearing his image, we live his risen life by the power of his life-giving Spirit, poured out at Pentecost – this is what Paul means whenever he talks of the 'spiritual'.

We therefore no longer live under the condemnation of the law, since we 'walk by the Spirit' (Galatians 5:16); sin has lost its power over us and death has lost its terror. When Jesus returns and this age finally passes away, the dead will be raised and whoever of us are alive at the time will also be transformed. The victory won in the cross and resurrection will finally be fulfilled, ushering in the promised new age of God's reign (Isaiah 25:8). What an inspiring hope to live by!

# 6 Raised to the life of the Spirit

**Romans 1:1–4; 4:23—5:2**

As we have seen Paul do elsewhere, he here includes the resurrection of Jesus as a central part of his short summary of his gospel. This is particularly significant in this letter, Paul's most systematic and developed presentation of what he believes, offered to a community that he himself did not help establish. As he did at the start of 1 Corinthians 15, he locates the good news about Jesus within the longer history of God's dealings with his people in the scriptures. This is the goal to which that story was always heading. Paul is clear that Jesus was fully human, and lived an 'earthly life' (1:3), but he says some striking things here about the importance of the resurrection.

The first is that Jesus' resurrection was not simply the experience of him as an individual – he does not rise from his own death but 'from the dead' (1:4), that is, from the realm of death and decay of this age which is passing away. It signals the beginning of a new age. Secondly, it doesn't just change the world; it changes Jesus too. This is the only time in his writing that Paul uses the word translated 'appointed' (1:4), and at first it might seem odd. Surely Jesus was already the Son of God, and the resurrection just revealed what he already was? No, says Paul: his resurrection brought about a decisive change, so that he is now 'the Son of God in power' (1:4), attaining fullness of relationship with the Father, as a result of which he received the 'name that is above every name' (Philippians 2:9), sharing with the Father his title of 'Lord'. Thirdly, Paul associates the Holy Spirit with Jesus' resurrection life; although he seems reluctant to claim that the Spirit raised Jesus, this new life is life in the Spirit – hence his use of 'spiritual' in 1 Corinthians 15.

Saving faith, then, is faith in the God who has done all this (4:24), in succession to the faith of Abraham and his descendants. Paul does not separate Jesus' death and resurrection, but sees them as a single act encompassing both forgiveness of sins and restoration to new life in fellowship with God. This is a life rooted in hope, but also one in which 'the love of God is poured into our hearts by his Spirit' (5:5).

## Guidelines

The resurrection of Jesus was clearly a central plank of belief in Jesus for Paul. Where Jesus' own proclamation centred on the kingdom of God (see Mark 1:16), it appears that Paul's proclamation centred on Jesus and his resurrection. This was the case even where such a message would have been a very strange idea indeed. In Acts 17:18 his listeners think he is talking about two new gods, one male and one female: Jesus and 'Anastasis' (the word for 'resurrection' in Greek, which is feminine). This illustrates both their puzzlement and Paul's commitment! But it leaves us with a question: is the resurrection as central in our faith and understanding as it was in Paul's? And is it as central in our conversation with others as it was for Paul?

This leads to another question of personal significance. Paul is clear that Jesus' resurrection demonstrates decisively that death has been defeated and that we have a good reason to hope – not with a general sense of optimism, but with robust confidence in God in the face of our mortality. We are right to grieve when we lose those close to us, or see tragic or untimely deaths – but we do not grieve as those without hope. So am I ready to face the reality of my own death, my own mortality, but to see it in the context of the hope that comes because of Jesus' resurrection promise?

But Paul is also clear this is not just a personal question. The resurrection signifies the breaking in of the new age, the age to come which we will only see fully revealed at Jesus' coming. According to Paul, this present age is passing away, and will be finally wrapped up when Jesus returns. So the resurrection equips us to live in a distinctive way, and means that our communities of faith are to model a new way of living. We should be people living the life of the future in the present. Am I living such a distinctive life, marching to a different drumbeat from the world around me? And am I encouraging my faith community to do the same? In what ways is the resurrection of Jesus leading us to model a new way of living and relating to others?

# 1 Under new command

**Romans 6:1–14**

The New Testament teaching about sin and forgiveness has often caused Christians problems – sometimes in quite different directions. In some traditions, sin is seen to be so serious (after all, it cost Jesus his life) that the Christian life is one long exercise in remorse and contrition. In others, sin is seen as relatively unimportant – after all, are we not now free from its penalty? And if

God loved us while we were sinners, surely he loves us still more now we are saved, even if we keep on sinning. We don't earn our salvation by being holy.

Paul cuts through these dilemmas by making a radical identification of Jesus' death and resurrection with the sacrament of baptism. Baptism has its origins in Jewish rites of purification, which were particularly associated with preparation for entry into the temple for offering sacrifice. Entering the water signified the desire to be cleansed of sin, and emerging (usually up separate steps) signified purity in preparation for worship. John the Baptist adapted this into a sign of once-for-all change, in readiness to follow the coming Messiah, and it then became the sign of initiation into Christian discipleship and a life of following Jesus.

Paul relates the two actions of baptism – submersion in the water and emergence from the water – to the paired actions of Jesus in his death and resurrection. Just as Jesus put an end to sin by his death, we renounce our life of sin as we 'die' in the water – the old life has now gone. And just as Jesus lived a new kind of life in his resurrection, we too begin a new life once we emerge from the water. (The connection between water, the Spirit and new life is also found in John 3:5.) Changing the metaphor, it is like moving from one dominion (under the authority of the ruler of this age, John 12:31, or the rule of sin) to another (under the rule or kingdom of God). Resurrection is our hope for the future, but it also signifies the pattern of new life we live now in Christ. Just as Jesus' resurrection was a decisive turning point for the world, so our baptism into his death and resurrection becomes a decisive and unrepeatable turning point for our lives – there is no going back to the life of sin.

# 2 The transition from death to life in the Spirit

**Romans 7:4–6; 8:9–11; 10:9**

In these three key passages in Romans, we see Paul making vital connections between resurrection, the law and the Spirit in Christian living. Paul is clear that the law given by God is a good thing (Romans 7:12; 1 Timothy 1:8) in that it sets out a healthy pattern of living that honours God. But for sinful humanity it merely succeeds in highlighting our sinfulness; it sets a standard and in doing so shows how we fail to live up to it; it becomes a 'law of sin and death' (Romans 8:2) since we cannot fulfil its demands. It explains holiness but cannot create holiness in us. By baptism we are now incorporated into Jesus, and into his death and resurrection, so that this old way of living has died in the waters of baptism and we are now living the resurrection life – the life of the age to come, life animated by the Spirit of God whose outpouring is the sign of the new age (Joel 2:28; Acts 2:17). The pattern of holy living set out in the law has not been abandoned, but our way of attaining it has. Now, we can start to live a holy life animated by the Spirit of God himself.

For Paul, this means we can now live the fruitful lives God intends for us. Paul has already contrasted the unfruitfulness of living without God in Romans 1 with the fruitfulness of Abraham and Sarah as they trusted God in chapter 4. Here he links such fruitfulness to living the resurrection life in the power of the Spirit, something we could not do previously. However, this resurrection life is, for now, just a foretaste. Our mortal bodies are still subject to death, living as we do in a fallen world, but our acquaintance with the life-giving power of the Spirit assures us that we will experience the fullness of life promised to those who trust in God. Salvation is offered to all those for whom Jesus is Lord. Jesus is the saving presence among us of the God of Israel (Paul changes *Yahweh* in Joel 2:32 to 'the Lord', meaning Jesus, when he quotes it in Romans 10:13). We trust in his resurrection not simply as a slogan, but as a lived reality.

# 3  Resurrection lives are cross-shaped

**2 Corinthians 4:7—5:5**

Paul's second letter to the Corinthians (of the ones that have survived, though it's actually the fourth he wrote) has quite a different feel from 1 Corinthians, and offers some of his most profound reflections on Christian discipleship and ministry. In it, he makes some fascinating new connections between the resurrection, suffering and Christian living.

In Ephesians 1:19–20, Paul talks of the 'incomparably great power for us who believe' which is the 'same mighty strength' by which God raised Jesus from the dead (compare 1 Corinthians 6:14), and he is clear that the Christian life is to be one of power (1 Corinthians 4:20, 2 Timothy 1:7). We might expect, then, that Paul's language about Christian ministry will be focused on the power, success and victory of the Christian life – but here we find the opposite! For Paul, ministry is about frustration, weakness and brokenness – so how can this be the foretaste of the resurrection life that we anticipate? The answer is that, paradoxically, the resurrection-shaped (anastiform) life is actually the cross-shaped (cruciform) life, because it is the life of Jesus.

Our natural human tendency is towards self-preservation and self-protection – and this is at no time greater than when we face the prospect of our own death. Luther described human sin as *cor curvum se*, the 'heart turned in on itself', a phrase which captures this tendency perfectly. But once we cross from death to life, from this human way of living into the resurrection life of Jesus, we no longer fear death or feel the need to preserve ourselves. Instead of turning in on ourselves, we are able to turn out towards others; instead of trying to preserve our lives, we are free to give them away. This is what Jesus taught and this is what Jesus did: in confidence that his Father would raise him, he was able to give his life away.

Paul is therefore not afraid of losing his life in ministry to others – in fact, this is the only sensible thing to do. Changing his analogy from 'body' (4:10, 11) to 'dwelling' (5:2, 4), he is happy for this earthly dwelling of his bodily life to be worn out and used up for others, since it bears no comparison to the dwelling God will provide in the resurrection.

# 4   United with Christ in service and glory

**Philippians 2:1–13**

Philippians is one of Paul's later letters; most scholars believe it was written in the early 60s during one of Paul's final periods of imprisonment. In it, he continues to develop the theme we explored in 2 Corinthians, that living a resurrection life frees us to give ourselves up for others. In this passage, the resurrection itself is not mentioned explicitly, but it forms the central hinge point of the great sweep of Jesus' life and ministry. In a statement reminiscent of the later poetry of the first chapter of John's Gospel, Paul is clear that Jesus shared the very nature of God prior to his incarnation – but that he gave up any sense of self-preservation in order to take human form. Paul sees the life and death of Jesus as a single movement of self-giving in obedience to the call of the Father, refusing to separate his incarnation, ministry and sacrificial death.

Because of Jesus' perfect faithfulness, therefore, the Father was faithful to him. Paul sums up the whole movement of resurrection, ascension and being seated at the right hand of the Father in the phrase 'exalted him to the highest place' (v. 9). We see this enacted spatially in the book of Revelation: there is One on the throne, but the Lamb, too, is on the very same throne, and they act in consort together as one. The 'name that is above every name' (v. 9) is the name of Israel's God (Isaiah 42:8), and 'every knee should bow... and every tongue acknowledge' (vv. 10–11) God alone, and no other (Isaiah 45:23) – Jesus is restored to sharing the glory of God that he was ready to let go of.

So, says Paul, being 'united with Christ' (v. 1) means that we too can rest in this hope of God's faithfulness – and it makes an immediate difference to how we relate to one another. Considering others better than ourselves is not about low self-esteem or being a doormat; it is about being ready to love and serve others, attending to their concerns without the need to protect our own position. It is as we live faithfully to this pattern of graciousness and generosity that we see in Jesus that we can rest in the faithfulness of God. 'Humble yourselves, therefore, under God's mighty hand, that he may lift you up in due time' (1 Peter 5:6).

# 5 Called to resurrection reality

**Philippians 3:7—4:1**

What we have read in Philippians 2 and earlier in 2 Corinthians 4 now enables us to make sense of Paul's dramatic language here. If resurrection life is about trusting God, and so being released to forsake self-protection and give ourselves away in love to others, then all the things that Paul was proud of prior to his encounter with Jesus on the Damascus road come to nothing. Worse than that – inasmuch as they tempt Paul to rely on what he has achieved, they are less than worthless, a dangerous distraction from the reality of life in Christ. Many translations blush at Paul's words, and suggest he calls these achievements 'garbage', or 'refuse' (3:8); the term he uses is actually much stronger than that! If we think any of our own achievements or credentials compare to the gift of life in Christ, they stink to high heaven and are only worth flushing away!

As he has done elsewhere, Paul holds together the paradox of the power of the resurrection with the suffering of the crucified one. He isn't suggesting that he is contributing to the atoning work of Christ, but that he is, as Jesus did, carrying his cross (Mark 8:34). This does not mean (as is commonly supposed) putting a brave face on during the general trials of life; it means constantly dying to self, letting go of our own concerns and being shaped and directed by the Spirit of God. It is this, and not the accumulation of religious merit badges, which is the path to resurrection by the faithfulness of God.

And Paul's description of this way of living is held in tension between the first resurrection and the last. God has demonstrated his power over life and death in the resurrection of Jesus, and it is by this that God has taken hold of us. God's decisive intervention has begun to change everything – but that change will not be completed until Jesus comes again, and the whole world is renewed. When Paul talks about being 'called... heavenwards' (3:14) or our 'citizenship which is in heaven', (3:20) he is not referring to escapism, but to living under God's rule – so that his name will be honoured and his will done as in heaven, so on earth.

# 6  Hope from beginning to end

**1 Timothy 3:14—4:5; 2 Timothy 2:8–13**

In his pastoral letters to Timothy, Paul is writing with an awareness that his ministry is drawing to a close as he nears the end of his life. Timothy has been Paul's companion for much of his ministry, and is co-author of six of his letters (2 Corinthians; Philippians; Colossians; 1 and 2 Thessalonians and Philemon); Paul has 'no one like him', and writes, 'as a son with his father he has served with me' (Philippians 2:22). The style of Paul's writing here is at times close to his style in Ephesians, which is not surprising since Timothy was from Anatolia (Turkey) and tradition suggests he became bishop of Ephesus.

In Paul's summaries of his teaching, written to encourage and equip Timothy as the baton of apostolic ministry passes to him, recognisable themes emerge. The first, in 1 Timothy 3:16, seems brief to the point of abruptness, but it has the familiar shape of the movement downwards and then upwards we saw in Philippians 2:5–6. 'Appeared' translates a semi-technical term for God's self-revelation, from which we get our word 'epiphany'; God came to us and revealed himself in the bodily, human life of Jesus. The phrase 'vindicated by the Spirit' is the closest Paul comes to suggesting that it was the Spirit of God who was at work in Jesus' resurrection, and it is clear that the gift of the Spirit at Pentecost was the sign that the promise of God to his people was fulfilled. The ascension completes Jesus' journey back to glory. Living in this pattern of incarnation–resurrection–glorification does not mean ascetic denial of this life, but redemption of it, so that we can receive all good gifts from God.

Even in Paul's final letter, the resurrection is just as central as it was in his earliest. The gospel for which he is chained holds the twin focuses of Jesus' humanity ('descended from David', 2 Timothy 2:8) and his vindication by God as Christ, the anointed one who brings God's kingdom life to us. Our identification with Jesus' death in the waters of baptism leads to life in him, beginning now but reaching completion when he comes to reign. As ever in Paul's writing, this remains a partnership between the irrevocable grace of God ('he remains faithful', 2 Timothy 2:13) and our willing response ('if we endure', 2 Timothy 2:12).

## Guidelines

Some church communities are very conscious of their own fragility and humanity, and aware that they do not have all the answers. This can often make them accessible, particularly for those who struggle with life. But this raises a question: God might understand my problems and challenges, but does he do anything to address them? Other churches are very conscious of the victory that God has won for us in Jesus' cross and resurrection, and have experienced God's presence helping them overcome their challenges, even to the point where they might claim that all their problems melt away. They are good at offering a sense of hope and change – but can seem inaccessible to many, because they make it look like church is for people who succeed in life.

Paul's understanding of resurrection that we have explored challenges both of these positions. The resurrection really does make a difference: it signals the end of the old way of life, the breaking in of the age to come, and it lifts us from death to life. It is striking how often Paul uses the language of power in relation to the resurrection – the demonstration of God's power in Jesus, but also the mighty working of that power in our lives. This brings transformation both for us and for those around us as we minister to one another by the power of the Spirit.

But for Paul the main thing that power brings is the strength to forget ourselves, to 'take up [our] cross' (Luke 9:23) and to follow Jesus. As we are released from sin and death, we live cruciform lives after the pattern of Jesus. The cross of Jesus does not just do something for us in putting sin to death, but it offers a pattern for us: the life of compassion and self-giving that we see in the Jesus of the Gospels. We should certainly know the victory that the resurrection brings into our lives, but the power of that victory allows us to face up to our own brokenness and wounds, and enables us to stand with the broken and the wounded, comforting them with the comfort that we ourselves have received (2 Corinthians 1:3–7).

# Colossians

The letter to the Colossians is full of Christ. It gives us one of the most sustained and exalted expositions of him in the New Testament, carefully applying the truth about him to practical Christian living.

The reason for its Christocentric focus is that there were believers in Colossae who hadn't grasped the heart of the Christian gospel sufficiently, and they were being attracted to another teaching that would corrupt it. Scholars differ over what that false teaching was, as will be explained later. Whatever it was, the Colossians were in danger of reducing Christ to one among many powers in their world. Even if they thought him powerful, he was not considered supreme. This letter is by way of preventative medicine, warning people to be wary lest false teaching seduces them away from their devotion to the pre-eminent Christ into full-blown heresy.

Some doubt whether Paul wrote Colossians, because of its style, its vocabulary and the developed nature of its theology. It parallels Ephesians in many respects, the Pauline authorship of which is widely, but not universally, questioned, and that reinforces the doubt about Colossians. There's no insurmountable reason for believing it is not genuinely Pauline, especially when we remember that Paul had not founded or visited the church himself. The author is writing to a group he does not personally know (2:1), except for Epaphras. Furthermore, they are responding to a particular concern that calls for a particular approach and vocabulary. We'll refer to the writer as Paul throughout.

The letter's readers were not professional theologians but sheep farmers, wool dyers and market traders. They lived insecure and precarious lives. Not only were they constantly on unsteady ground financially, but they also lived in an earthquake zone. Moreover, the River Lycus, which ran through the town, although very beneficial in enabling them to produce excellent-quality wool, could also be bad-tempered and had been known to threaten destruction of the town through floods. In the gospel they had discovered a secure foundation in a powerful Christ, against all their malicious enemies. Paul warns them not to trade that in for less-secure spiritual foundations.

Whatever the unknowns about this letter, hopefully our faith in Christ will be greatly enriched by what it teaches.

Quotations are from the New International Version (Anglicised).

# 1 Thanking God

**Colossians 1:1–8**

Paul's letter begins in a conventional way with him introducing himself and Timothy as its writers, and sending greetings to the Christians in Colossae. Colossae was a little town on the River Lycus, known for its wool trade. It had seen better days and was overshadowed by nearby Laodicea and Hierapolis. Colossae was the geographical location of the Colossian Christians, but their real identity was shaped by their spiritual location 'in Christ' (v. 2)

Conventionally, the letter starts with thankfulness. But Paul's thanksgiving is more than conventional. He attributes every cause of thanksgiving to the living God – not an amorphous deity but the God revealed through his son Jesus – who has brought about the blessings he celebrates (v. 3). Good things didn't just happen and were neither attributable to fate nor to any of the other 'powers' that are going to concern him shortly, but to God alone.

It would be difficult to press more of the great words of the Christian faith into a prayer of thanksgiving than Paul does here. The familiar triad of *faith, love and hope* (vv. 4–5) is at the heart of it. These resulted from the Colossians' response to the truth and the preaching of the *gospel* (good news) about Jesus, which led them to experience God's *grace* – his unearned and undeserved favour and forgiveness (v. 6). Other religious groups may look more impressive than this small group of Christ-followers, but in reality they are part of a worldwide movement which is developing and transforming lives everywhere (v. 6). All these words cluster around Jesus of Nazareth, who is astonishingly spoken of as the *Lord*: the title Jewish folk gave to God, and Gentiles gave to Caesar. Powerful indeed. He is also *Christ*, the long-awaited Messiah who would usher in the new age.

Paul is not so captivated by these great words that he is unmindful of the human messenger who brought the gospel to Colossae. Epaphras (v. 7) was probably converted to Christ when Paul preached in Ephesus, and took the good news back to his own hometown, resulting in the Christian group to whom Paul is now writing. They are a gospel community who are Paul's spiritual grandchildren.

# 2 Non-stop praying

**Colossians 1:9–14**

Again, typical of an ancient letter, after expressing thanks, Paul states his desire for his readers in a prayer. Every phrase is rich in background and carefully chosen to address their situation. We can only pick up a few threads here.

He prays for knowledge and wisdom (v. 7) since they prize wisdom (2:23) but are searching for it in the wrong place. Wisdom is found in Christ (2:3) and revealed by the Holy Spirit (v. 9), not in religious rules and human philosophies. That wisdom should colour their conversations with each other, as Paul himself practises (1:28; 3:16). Having already mentioned the fruitfulness of the gospel (1:6), Paul mentions that the fruit he longs to see in them is 'good works' (v. 10), which will show evidence that their lives are consistent with the gospel they believe. A third thread is thankfulness, which Paul encourages in 2:7; 3:15, 17 and 4:2. Here, Paul's requests are not a list of demands but clothed with 'joyful thanks to the Father' (v. 12), not for the Colossians so much as for God's rescuing of them from darkness.

That leads to the next major aspect of this prayer, the theme of power. The Colossians fear the powers of unseen spiritual forces. Paul prays that they may be 'strengthened with all power according to his glorious might' (v. 11). He has in mind the power of God who brought creation into existence from nothing, and the power that raised Jesus from the dead as well. Though, surprisingly, this power is not with a view to them dazzling others with miracles or conquering the world, but so that they might patiently endure. It's a short step from this to Paul mentioning that people inevitably live under one of two competing power regimes (vv. 12–13). He uses the words 'dominion' and 'kingdom' to describe them. People are never autonomous and self-sufficient, but always owe allegiance to greater powers. One brings darkness and captivity. The other – that of the Son of God – brings liberty and forgiveness. Paul rejoices that the Colossians have come under the rule of Christ, even if, as yet, they haven't totally understood its full implications and are not appreciating that Jesus is to be their sole sovereign. No matter: that's what Paul will explain in the rest of the letter.

# 3 Jesus is supreme

Verses 15–20 are often thought of as a pre-existing hymn which Paul inserts, and perhaps adapts, because of its relevance. It contains the most stunning claims about Jesus, 'the Son', viewing him from an eternal and cosmic perspective as the supreme one over all (v. 18). It's amazing that such claims are made of a man who, not many years before, people knew as a flesh-and-blood carpenter's son from Nazareth.

As 'the image of the invisible God' (v. 15), Jesus is what Adam was meant to be (Genesis 1:27) before his destiny was marred by his disobedience. Jesus is a uniquely perfect human being. Yet, for all his humanity, he's in a class of his own. Being 'firstborn over all creation' (v. 15) means he's like a firstborn son, in the place of supreme honour, rather than he was born before others. Creation came into being by his agency and for his glory. He plays a continuing role in creation, holding it all together, so that it is neither anarchic nor chaotic (vv. 16–17). Its continuing existence and order depends on him. The Colossians may fear other powers, seen and unseen, and have several names for them (thrones, powers, rulers, authorities) but Jesus surpasses them all. Therefore, he alone is the one to whom reverent submission should be shown.

But, they might respond, if that's how it started, creation now seems to be going to rack and ruin, as the constant disruption of life and the reality of death reminds them. True, except God is working towards a new creation, using the church as its harbinger. We can be confident of this because Christ overcame death and pioneered the way to a new creation through his own resurrection (v. 18). No one is ahead of him in the renewed creation which one day will be fully healed.

Two things make all this possible. Firstly, who Jesus is: more than a man, he is God in human form (v. 19; 2:9). Secondly, what Jesus did: this astonishing renewal is taking place because he died on a cross (v. 20). God conquers death, destruction and evil powers by embracing them in the crucifixion and then, through the resurrection, demonstrating just how much stronger he is than any force which opposes him or threatens our peace.

# 4 Paul's ministry

From the grand vista of the supreme Christ (1:15–23), Paul now turns to write of his own ministry. The hinge is found in verse 23 where he speaks of himself as a 'servant' of the gospel he has been celebrating. His service involves a close identity with Christ in that he too undergoes physical suffering (1:24–25), but he is up for it because God has unmistakably commissioned him to break out of the confines of the Jewish world and bring the good news of a Jewish Messiah, the Lord of all, to a Gentile world (1:26–27). His ministry requires extraordinary efforts, not least because the message is so contrary to the normal understanding of religion and philosophy (2:1–5).

At the centre of these reflections lies a concise statement of Paul's life's mission. Verses 28–29 speak of his message ('He is the one we proclaim'), namely the Christ whom he has introduced and will speak of further in the letter – the historical flesh-and-blood man who was actually also God incarnate, who died and rose again for our salvation. Speaking of him involves various methods of communication, sometimes 'proclaiming' where the news is unknown, sometimes 'admonishing' where there is error and sometimes 'teaching' where there is ignorance. Wisdom, as mentioned, is one of the great concerns of the Colossians. Paul uses it in a different way to say that his manner is neither foolish nor arrogant, but prudent, which at least means his speech is 'seasoned with grace' (4:5–6). His purpose is not to build his own empire, create his own disciples, keep people dependent on him or merely give them a happy time, but to 'present everyone fully mature in Christ'. He's aiming for spiritual adults who will be his glory on the day of judgement (1 Thessalonians 2:19). The statement concludes with a neatly balanced recognition that such a calling requires maximum human effort but not unaided human effort. The energy Paul expends on his mission is that which 'Christ so powerfully works in me'. Without that spirit-fuelled approach to mission, he would, as many can today testify, experience burnout pretty quickly, or be so discouraged by opposition that he'd give up.

# 5 Continue

Our culture puts a huge premium on novelty. Our education system prizes 'original' research at the expense of old wisdom. Our shopping is geared to 'new, improved' products, which suffer conveniently from 'built-in obsolescence'. As far as continuing sales are concerned, progress is key.

This is not just a modern disease. When it came to spiritual experience the Colossians, like others, were restless about what they had encountered of God and been taught about Jesus, and they were searching for something more, something different, something new to satisfy their longings. The core of Paul's message, introduced first in 1:23 and reinforced more thoroughly in today's reading, is to stick with what they have already received in the gospel of Jesus Christ. Using vocabulary from three different spheres of life he urges them not to deviate from the message of the gospel. Employing an agricultural picture, he encourages their rootedness. Organic growth depends on roots going down into the soil. Don't keep digging them up and transplanting them elsewhere. That will kill them. Using construction language, he encourages the Colossians to build up their lives on the foundation of Christ. You don't stop building as soon as the foundations are laid. The point of them is to build on them. Although somewhat hidden by our English translations, next Paul uses commercial language to urge them to confirm their commitment to Christ. The word translated 'strengthened' (NIV) or 'established' (NRSV) in verse 7 was used when a transaction in the marketplace was confirmed. So he exhorts them not to look for a new message but to develop the one they've already received.

Other messages, based on human traditions and pseudo-philosophies, were beginning to appeal to the Colossians. But they shouldn't be fooled as these don't have anything to offer. The problem is his readers haven't fully grasped just who Jesus was and how great his salvation is. 'The fullness of the deity' uniquely lived in the man from Nazareth. He wasn't just more godly than the rest of us; he was God. There was nothing deficient in, omitted from or lacking in him. It is both impossible and unnecessary to supplement or improve on his work of salvation in any way. Stick, Paul pleads, to the original gospel and don't go after novelties. Your need is not for something new, but to understand the old gospel more fully.

# 6 The all-conquering cross

Using a somewhat novel, and sometimes puzzling, approach, these verses draw us to the heart of the gospel. One thing seems to lead to another as Paul explains the decisive impact of Christ's physical – physicality is stressed throughout – death and resurrection on the destructive powers that his readers feared, and on the believers themselves.

Paul starts, unusually, with circumcision (v. 11). Without Christ, his readers were functionally uncircumcised, whether Jews or Gentiles (v. 13). Now in Christ they have undergone the circumcision of the heart commanded in Jeremiah 4:4. Paul seems to view Christ's crucifixion as a form of circumcision whereby his whole life, not just the foreskin, was stripped away. Authentic followers of Christ will have experienced the same, treating their former way of life as dead to them. Paul then follows the more regular pattern of Romans 6:1–4 to explain that the Colossians have been joined with Christ by undergoing the burial of their pre-Christ lives, captured in the symbolism of being submerged in water in baptism, and by sharing in his new resurrection life (v. 12).

The result of their identification with Christ is twofold: forgiveness and freedom from debt (vv. 13–14). Both ideas were introduced in 1:14. Forgiveness removes any obstacle to their becoming citizens of King Jesus, while redemption is the payment of a price to secure their freedom from the kingdom of darkness. Their failure to keep God's law put them in debt to God – a debt they could never repay from their own resources – and so condemned them. Someone else needed to pay it for them.

So Paul speaks of the cross as achieving two things. Firstly, it settled the debt. The writ of condemnation was cancelled as Jesus nailed it to the cross, just as Pilate nailed the ironic indictment of Jesus as King of the Jews to his literal cross (John 19:19–22). Secondly, the crucifixion that looked like a defeat was in fact a victory. To the outward eye, Jesus was stripped naked, rendered powerless and made an object of derision. In reality, God was turning the tables on all the destructive, evil forces that kept people in subjection. In total weakness God was, in fact, disarming and defeating the enemy. At Calvary, the true eye perceives not Christ the victim but Christ the victor, conquering all.

# Guidelines

Colossians has introduced us to some great themes concerning Jesus, the Messiah, which have immense implications for our contemporary world.

The Colossians were conscious of evil powers that were intent on destroying them or robbing them of their freedom. These powers were both seen and unseen, external and within, located in institutions and in the spirit world. Why is it that the Western church, unlike the church in the rest of the world, doesn't seem too conscious of such powers?

Unlocking creation – past, present and future – meant understanding Christ rather than resorting to exclusively scientific or pseudo-scientific explanations. How are such views compatible?

Paul's life's mission was set out in 1:28–29. How would you define your life's mission?

In a world of religious pluralism, Paul's message of the supremacy and exclusivity of Christ may seem uncomfortable. How can we present this message graciously but without compromise?

This letter contains a somewhat unusual view of the accomplishments of the cross, often known as *Christus Victor*. How central is this explanation of the atonement to our thinking and worship?

Above all, this week's readings should lead us to worship Jesus as Lord. Use a classic hymn that speaks of Jesus and use it as the basis for further meditation on the glory of Christ. Suitable hymns, among others, might be: 'Christ triumphant, ever reigning'; 'Come let us worship the Christ of creation!'; 'Crown him with many crowns'; 'How sweet the name of Jesus sounds'; 'Join all the glorious names'; 'Meekness and majesty, Manhood and Deity' and 'Name of all majesty'.

23–29 April

# 1 Dying and reigning with Christ

## Colossians 2:16—3:4

At long last we get some indication of the false teaching which Paul and Epaphras were concerned might undermine the pure gospel of Jesus Christ. The description of it, however, is not altogether clear and has given rise to major debates.

Older views suggested it was an early form of Gnosticism – an ancient religious worldview that taught a strong division between the real spiritual world and the evil material world. Salvation lay in secret knowledge and in kindling the inner spark of divinity in us all. In using words like 'wisdom' and 'fullness' and 'shadow', Paul seems to be engaging with Gnostic teaching and his stress on the physical nature of Christ, in contrast to Gnostic views of the material world, points in the same direction.

Some elements of the false teaching, however, seem to come directly out of Judaism, particularly that strain of it which was to be found among the Jewish Diaspora. They were not only known for their practice of food laws and sabbath observance, and for their religious regulations, but they were also known to have incorporated angels into their worship (v. 18). Yet other elements, like the use of 'disqualify' and the reference to visionary experiences (also v. 18), possibly point in the direction of the mystery religions.

Clinton Arnold's recent suggestion that the false teaching was probably some form of folk religion where several streams of religious practice were mixed together in an impure form, has most to commend it. Not only does he produce supporting evidence about this mix-and-match form of religion (see *The Colossian Syncretism*), but it is true to experience. Many worshippers are syncretistic in their religious beliefs and practice.

Uncertainty about the troublesome teaching should not distract us from what Paul says is the important truth. Spiritual disciplines may vary in their degree of helpfulness but ultimately they do nothing to cure the problem of sin (v. 23). For that there is only one answer, which is found not in religious shadows but in the real Christ (v. 17), the one he introduced in 1:15–20, not the Christ of our imagination. Our only hope of dealing with 'sensual indulgence' lies in our identification with him by dying (v. 20) and rising with him (3:1–4), which, as Paul will explain, means putting to death our sinful lifestyles and realising personally the new life Christ has secured through his resurrection.

# 2 Execute… execute

## Colossians 3:5–11

What does it mean to die with Christ? Part of the answer lies in 'crucifying' patterns of behaviour that are incompatible with God's moral character. Sadly, execution by crucifixion was a common feature of the Roman world and Paul's readers would have readily understood his call. Crucifixion was a decisive event in which the condemned person ended up dead, even if it took some time for the victim to die. Paul calls on Christians to adopt the same decisive attitude to ungodly ways of living. There should be no half-heartedness in dealing with the problem.

His approach, typical of ancient moral writings, is to provide a list of vices (virtues will come later) that should be removed from his readers' lives, like the rubbish we put out for the refuse collectors. Two lists are given (vv. 5, 8) which cover everything from internal emotions like lust and anger to external actions like sexual immorality and lying. He connects greed and idolatry (v. 5) in a standard Jewish way, because wanting something greedily is to make it an object of worship, and so fundamentally to betray the living God. One reason to avoid such behaviour, apart from it being inherently self-destructive, is that God is angry at such vices and will hold people accountable if they commit them (v. 6). From the Bible's beginning to its end, there can be no avoiding the wrath of God as something that is real, terrifying and still to come, even if it has already started. Read more in Romans 1:18–31.

This teaching is essentially relational. The vices all undermine trust, erode good relationships and make fellowship impossible. By contrast, Christians are being built into a new godly community, free from prejudice and without divisive distinctions of any kind, whether ethnic, religious or social (in Galatians 3:28 Paul adds gender). The positive news is that Christians are being reconstructed, so that God's original desire for a humanity that reflected his image is restored in them (v. 10). That can only be done in relationship. But the first step to the 'new self' is to deal with the 'old self' by getting rid of it.

If the Daleks in BBC's *Doctor Who* are known for saying, 'Exterminate… Exterminate…' Christians should be known for saying, 'Execute… execute…' – not others, but self-centred ways of living.

# 3 Balanced Christianity

**Colossians 3:12–17**

If you've ever finished a dirty job and been glad to strip off your soiled clothes, stand in the shower and then dress in clean clothes, you'll get the sense of what Paul teaches here. The image in his mind, however, might well be what happened after baptism when the person confessing faith would take off their wet garments and dress themselves in fresh ones. Our dirty rags need discarding (vv. 5–11), but being 'in Christ' is about more than what we stop doing or being. It is a positive message about becoming like the Christ whom we follow. We've a new 'uniform' to put on.

Paul points out some of the features of this new wardrobe. Some garments relate to our personal character, like those of compassion, kindness, humility and not holding grudges (vv. 12–13). Love is presented as either the belt that holds everything together or the overcoat that covers all the rest (v. 14). That must be our everyday wear. We probably spend quite a bit of time thinking about what to wear when we go out with others. Likewise, Paul instructs us to be careful what we wear when we're out and about in the Christian community. Peace, not arguing; thankfulness (mentioned twice for emphasis), not grumbling; scripture ('the message of Christ', v. 16), not our own ideas; and worship, not gossip or idle chat must be our primary clothing (vv. 15–16). And just as our clothes send out signals about who we are, so this set of garments must not be put on just for effect but genuinely reflect our true natures and ambitions – what is 'in your hearts' as Paul puts it (v. 15).

We are required to get rid of vices, but we're not left naked. We are also required to cultivate virtues. 'Taking off' is followed by 'putting on'. 'Do not' is balanced by 'Do', in the power of Christ. The same balance is found in the longer version of this teaching in Ephesians 4:25—5:20. We all have a tendency to emphasise one or other of these twin poles. But both are necessary.

# 4 'In the Lord'

## Colossians 3:18—4:1

The basic social unit of the ancient world was the household. It was composed of an intergenerational family at its core, unmarried relatives, slaves and associated workers. Given its importance, ancient philosophers and ethicists gave some attention to how relationships within the family should be regulated, and Paul, once again, adopts a conventional approach to dealing with the issue. What difference would being a Christian family make from being a family whose religious identity was shaped by the worship of other deities?

Superficially, Paul's instructions seem very conservative – as some have argued strongly – and give little room for any dramatic social change to take place. Paul shapes his 'household code', as it was called, around the three traditional relationships of husband–wife, parent–child and master–slave. The chief authority figure in the household was the husband or master, and Paul seems to reinforce their position. But a closer reading shows these instructions contain a radical heart even if it is covered in conventional flesh. Husbands are not told to make their wives submit, but wives are voluntarily invited to submit to their husbands, 'as is fitting in the Lord' (v. 18). Husbands are to have affection and sensitivity to their wives, not be authoritarian towards them. The longer version of this code in Ephesians 5:21—6:33 brings out the mutual submission of husbands and wives even more.

In contrast to other household codes, children, remarkably, are addressed in their own right and, while their obedience is enjoined, the corresponding instruction to their fathers, the educators in the family, circumscribes the behaviour of the latter greatly. The fullest instructions are reserved for slaves, perhaps because there were a lot of them in the church. Some of them may have assumed that being brothers and sisters in Christ rendered the need to respect their master or conform to their expected social role unnecessary. Paul instructs them not to be presumptuous and puts their work in the wider context of worshipping God. Then, in an unprecedented way, masters have their wings clipped by being told they have a master to whom they are accountable as well.

Once you inject the faith of Jesus into these household instructions, the nature of them changes radically. At every point their pattern for relationships has to be governed by the radical teaching of Christ. While it seems that nothing changes, the truth is, everything changes.

# 5  Final encouragements

**Colossians 4:2–6**

The conclusions to Paul's letters are more than a convenient way of bringing the correspondence to a close, and here the further instructions are spiritually rich, repeating some familiar themes and introducing new ones.

The major new issue is prayer. In encouraging the Colossians to 'devote' themselves to prayer, Paul is hinting that prayer is always something of a battle that requires determination (v. 2). A few verses later (v. 12), in commending Epaphras's prayer life, Paul recognises prayer is more like a wrestling match than a stroll in the park. This sense of conflict carries over to his advice to his readers to be vigilant, constantly on guard against the enemy. Being watchful is exactly what Jesus expects of his disciples (Mark 13:5–23; 14:32–42). Having begun his letter by praying for them (1:9–13), he asks them now to pray for the believers (v. 3). He doesn't ask for prayer for his health, or for freedom from opposition and discomfort (as we often pray today), but for opportunities to spread the good news of Jesus the Messiah courageously. Prayer is one of the most important ways in which we can serve one another.

The second new element is the awareness that there is a boundary between Christians and others; there are believers and unbelievers, insiders and outsiders. It is self-evident that Paul expects the Colossians to share their faith with others, and to know what and why they believe. He's more concerned that they should share it graciously and wisely, both in their actions and their words (vv. 5–6). How easy it is for zealous, well-meaning, evangelistic Christians to lack the basic qualities of humility and sensitivity.

The familiar themes are those of thankfulness and, as mentioned, wisdom, which Paul has referred to in 1:9, 28; 2:3, 23; 3:16. Thankfulness (v. 2) stops prayer from becoming a shopping list of wants from God. It is the sixth time he's mentioned it in this short letter (1:3, 12; 2:7; 3:15, 17), which either indicates the Colossians needed to overcome a culturally negative mindset and a grumbling disposition, or simply that it is extremely important for any Christian, whatever their temperament, to give thanks. Thankfulness is a healthy spiritual discipline, but it is extraordinary that we even need it to be a discipline. After all, in Christ we have so much for which to be thankful.

# 6 The new community in action

Paul may have been a driven, pioneering personality, and so task-orientated that he wasn't the easiest person to get on with. Yet we never see him working alone, and his letters display what warm relations he had with his fellow missionary travellers. Colossians 4:7–18 gives some fascinating pen portraits of one such group.

Look at what it says about Tychicus (v. 7). Paul invents words like *syn-doulos*, meaning fellow servant, to describe how he values him. Paul is always using the prefix *syn-* in his letters – as in fellow worker, fellow servant and fellow prisoner – to reflect a non-hierarchical way of working together with his team. Tychicus is acting here as the postman, delivering the letter to Colossae. Onesimus had run away from Colossae as an untrustworthy fugitive slave (see Philemon) but has now become 'our faithful and dear brother' (v. 9). He is a prime example of the transformation the gospel can work in someone's life. Aristarchus was so committed to the mission that he is in prison with Paul (v. 10). Having fallen out earlier with John Mark, according to Acts 15:36–41, Paul is now reconciled with him and they are pulling together (vv. 10–11). Reading between the lines, Epaphras, the original evangelist to Colossae (1:7) and its intercessor, may have been subject to some criticism (vv. 14–15), so Paul commends his maturity and stamina. Of Jesus Justus, we only know what's here (v. 11). We can learn much about doctor Luke, the supreme artist with words, from his own writings (v. 14). Demas (v. 14) sadly subsequently went off the rails (2 Timothy 4:10). Archippus is told for some reason to finish what he started (v. 17).

The sense of belonging extends from this group of individuals to relationships between the churches, as we see here from the reference to the nearby church of Laodicea (vv. 15–16). There is no such thing as an 'independent church' in the New Testament. We should also note that the Laodicean church, like most at the time, met in a house, not an ecclesiastical building. It would have been a relatively, even if modestly, wealthy house with the houseowner playing a major role in church leadership. At Laodicea, the leader is a woman called Nympha.

What a mixed bag Paul's team were. What a wonderful variety of people, backgrounds and gifts. There's no room for individualism and independence. Here's an illustration of the new community Christ creates through his gospel.

## Guidelines

In the second part of Paul's Colossian letter, he spells out the implications of the supremacy, and supreme victory, of Christ for the way his followers shape their daily lives. If Christ is true wisdom, then his followers should live wisely. If Christ is all Paul claims he is, then several things follow:

- False teaching and syncretistic religious practices should be rejected, however immediately attractive they might appear to be.
- Lives should be lived in the light of Christ's death and resurrection, to which Christians are joined in their own experience.
- A rigorous commitment to do away with sinful ways of living and to em-

brace new qualities found in Christ is called for.

- They should be a new, united community, a foretaste of the new creation, which shuns individualism.
- They should embrace their existing social roles but live differently within them, because Christ would be governing all their behaviour and relationships.
- They should aim for godliness in prayer, watchfulness against temptation and prudence in relating to non-Christians with a humble confidence in the gospel.
- They will be a thankful people, free from grumbling and fear.
- They should relate to each other with the quality of love and delight Paul shows in his fellow workers.

That's not a bad list to use as a personal spiritual check-up or as a health check for our churches. Please use this list for personal prayer and reflection, being careful, of course, to follow it up with action where appropriate.

---

**FURTHER READING**

Clinton Arnold, *The Colossian Syncretism* (Wipf & Stock, 2014).

Andrew T. Lincoln, 'The Letter to the Colossians', *New Interpreter's Bible*, XI, Leander E. Keck (ed.) (Abingdon Press, 2000).

Douglas Moo, *The Letters to the Colossians and to Philemon* (Pillar New Testament Commentaries) (Apollos, 2008).

Derek Tidball, *The Reality is Christ, The Message of Colossians for Today* (Christian Focus, 1999).

N.T. Wright, *Colossians and Philemon* (Tyndale New Testament Commentary) (IVP, 1986).

# Science fiction: culture and faith

Christianity is an incarnated faith, but are we an incarnated people? Are we fully present and engaged in the culture we live in, and what is our response to it? To take the classic five responses that theologian H. Richard Niebuhr detected in scripture and Christian history, and presented in *Christ and Culture*: are we dead against our culture? Do we promote or even idolise it? Do we stand above it, commandeering its preferred features? Do we take the tensions of faith and culture as paradoxical? Or do we seek to transform our culture? We have things to learn from people who are at home in each of these responses. But our faith is an incarnated faith, and we are 'in the world but not of the world' (compare John 17:15); we are not just placed in this tension, but challenged to live in this culture and age as agents of change and transformation, 'that the world may believe' (John 17:21).

Our age is dominated by media. Old media continue, of course: print, theatre, cinema, radio and TV; and new media proliferate: the internet, mobile phones and social media. And the place of drama as a medium of entertainment, information, engagement and community grows. The telling of dramatic stories not only entertains, but also shapes and defines people and culture. Science fiction is one influential genre today. With its combination of mythic scope and future hopes and fears in its stories, it engages with the deepest questions – and here lies our context, for we tell stories with transcendent glory to shape our future, and our present: 'heavenly stories with an earthly meaning' and not just 'earthly stories with a heavenly meaning'.

The most searching questions of science fiction turn out to be spiritual ones. We begin with the most familiar – 'Are we alone in the universe?' We engage with these questions through scripture, reflection and prayer, the better to connect with the underlying spiritual search of our times, and the people touched by this search.

Quotations are from the New International Version (Anglicised).

# 1 Are we alone?

**Genesis 1:1–27**

Science fiction frequently drives us back to the theology of creation, and therefore to Genesis and the Psalms. We ask, 'Why are we here? How are we made? What is really distinctive about humanity? How do we fit in to the universe – as a species, and personally?' And, of course, 'Are we fundamentally alone in the universe?'

The latter is the classic question of science fiction, but it is a spiritual question. And the spiritual question is more fundamental. To discover a new world and sentient beings is interesting. But it does not resolve the existential question. The intention 'to explore strange new worlds, to seek out new life and new civilizations, to boldly go where no man has gone before', as the original *Star Trek* series put it, imagined new planets and new peoples within them. But Europeans had already discovered 'new worlds' – the Americas in 1493, and Australasia in 1770. However, the discovery of these peoples did not resolve humanity's existential isolation.

We are of course not alone: we live in a world awash with life (vv. 20–25). Genesis 2 also narrates how 'it is not good for the man to be alone' (v. 18), and God creates a partner for him, the woman. But even this does not resolve human isolation, a mystery we are reminded of in the saying, 'You can be alone in a crowd.'

We are made in the image of God (vv. 26–27), but what does that mean? The text does not state the answer, but the question is vital, and Christians have long wrestled with it. Among the responses to this, Robert Jenson in his *Systematic Theology* notes that, unlike the rest of creation, we are *addressed* by God. Fundamentally, we are not alone: 'In the beginning, God...' (v. 1). And, as Augustine of Hippo famously noted, God has made us in such a way that we don't know ourselves until we know him, and know ourselves as known by him. The universe lives in us, and to know the Creator of the universe living in us is to realise we are truly not alone.

# 2 Are we unique?

Genesis 1:26—2:3

The concluding great act of creation in Genesis 1 sees the formation of humanity, male and female, in the image of God (vv. 26–27), setting the scene for the world as we know it, with humanity in stewardship of the created order (vv. 28–30). To this, science fiction poses some potentially disturbing questions: 'What if, one day, we discovered aliens, advanced beings from another world, either as advanced as humanity or more advanced? Would the discovery of such aliens subvert Christian beliefs? Are we unique?'

The psalmist talks of an imaginary journey into the heavens (whether taken as the skies, or the spiritual realms), and then affirms that even on such a journey, we can know God's presence there (Psalm 139:7–12) – as the first humans behind the moon, aboard Apollo 8, found, leading crewmen William Anders, James Lovell and Frank Borman to read movingly from Genesis 1:1–10 on Christmas Eve, 1968. However, the Bible does not talk of alternative planetary worlds, and does not engage in speculation about life on other worlds. But for us, these have been live questions for half a millennium. Less than a generation after Columbus discovered the 'New World', Thomas More wrote his famous *Utopia* (1516), imagining a fantastical people different from what had been known, and challenging contemporary assumptions.

C.S. Lewis, in his allegorical science fiction Cosmic Trilogy (1938, 1943 and 1945) could imagine Venus and Mars as worlds in which God might relate to its peoples as unfallen. And some more adventurous Christian songwriters have speculated in their lyrics about other planets on which the Lord would also be crucified for its God-fearing beings – as in Sydney Carter's song 'Every star shall sing a carol' and Larry Norman's 'UFO'. Would the Lord indeed act for them as for us? Or would our mandate to go into all the world (Matthew 28:20) one day include other worlds?

However, as Wolfhart Pannenberg reminds us in his *Systematic Theology*, the Bible does actually speak of beings more advanced than us, namely angels, who need no redemption, or else have rebelled and are incapable of it.

# 3 Who are you?

Matthew 4:1–11

The 1990s science fiction series *Babylon 5* pivoted on two fundamental questions: 'Who are you?' and 'What do you want?' Its creator and main writer Joe Straczynski saw that the way and the sequence in which we answer these two questions shapes us. Early on in that epic five-year series, the question 'What do you want?' gets put to many ambassadors of the galactic powers, and when one of these, Londo of the Centauri, finally spits out his answer – that he wants the glory days of the empire back – the agent putting the question knows he has his man. Dark forces are unleashed and millions if not billions of people are destroyed, because what Londo wants controls him. Desire controls his identity. And that way lies tragedy.

Jesus, in the desert temptations, gets this question put to him three times, if more indirectly. '*What do you want?* Bread?' Jesus answers this by showing that he knows who he is: he is the Son of God, and therefore hungers after God's word. '*What do you want?* Fame? As the one who jumped from the temple and was saved by angels?' But again, Jesus is secure as the Son of God, even when the devil quotes scripture: he is the Son of God and so seeks God's will. '*What do you want?* Power – all the power in the world?' It is the classic distortion of a Messiah, one who rules the world. Surely he would be 'great David's greater Son' if all nations were subject to him. '*What do you want, Jesus?*' But again, Jesus knows he is the Son of God. He seeks God, and will worship him alone.

Who are you? Who am I? How many of us desire sustenance, approval and power, whether in the sphere of the church, or the workplace, or in our family? We need to face the 'What do you want?' questions in the context of knowing who we are: we are those who are 'in Christ'. Jesus defines us. 'Therefore, there is now no condemnation for those who are in Christ Jesus' (Romans 8:1). 'You are a chosen people, a royal priesthood, a holy nation, God's special possession' (1 Peter 2:9).

# 4 What is the evil we face?

**Revelation 12:1—13:1**

Science fiction is drama, and central to much of it is conflict with evil. Evil takes many forms, and science fiction written for children and the family, like *Doctor Who*, often paints evil in primary colours, with the megalomaniac, the capricious monster and the weapon running amok, threatening death on an apocalyptic scale.

But is the apocalyptic of the Bible the grandfather of all this, or very different? Now, scriptural apocalyptic to modern eyes is full of dramatic, even lurid imagery, and is often taken as baffling. But it is *apocalyptic*, that is, it is *revealing*, which is the meaning of the root word in Greek. And what it reveals is what God is doing, hidden from the world at large, but sometimes visible to believers, just as Elisha's servant Gehazi was shown the invisible army defending them (2 Kings 6:17). This is the heart of the book of Revelation – a 'revelation... to show... what must soon take place' (Revelation 1:1). Here, John sees the Lord in glory, who was dead, but is alive (Revelation 1:18). Then he is shown the truth about the seven churches (Revelation 1:20—3:22). Next revealed is 'a door standing open in heaven' (Revelation 4:1), showing heaven as the prophets were shown it, where the holiness of God echoes with praises (see Isaiah 6:1–8; Ezekiel 1:1–28). Then, crucially, John sees heaven transformed, from the time when no one was worthy to open the scroll (Revelation 5:3), to when 'a Lamb, looking as if it had been slain... took the scroll', prompting new praises, because Jesus, the 'Lamb who was slain', is worthy to open the scroll (Revelation 5:9).

In our world, evil really puts up a fight, and people suffer terrible consequences. But hidden from the world, there is 'war in heaven' (v. 7), in which Satan is being defeated (v. 9). So here on earth, evil, suffering and death seem inescapable, and we recognise the cry of Job (e.g. Job 14:1–22). But seemingly invisibly, God is working for good (Romans 8:28); the apparent victory of despots, including the ultimate villain, Satan, is illusory. God will win.

# 5 Is human evil unchangeable?

**Acts 26:1–32**

Good science fiction often provides a searching study of evil – not just the evil of monsters, like the Daleks or Cybermen of *Doctor Who*, but the evil within human beings. For many, the best-written story of *Doctor Who* was 'The Caves of Androzani' (1984), which well illustrates human evil in its different forms. Apart from the cruder evil of gun-runners, casual military brutality and political opportunism, we have the cold, calculating evil of magnate Trau Morgus, and the hot, angry evil of his nemesis Sharaz Jek. The same contrast lies at the heart of the *Star Wars* series, with the calculating deceit of Emperor Palpatine, and the more obviously villainous Darth Vader. But in *Return of the Jedi* (1983), Vader, surprisingly, proves capable of repentance.

Some people are committed to their self-centred vision of the world, and whatever the consequences, they stick to it. It is remarkable how dictators, even when facing certain defeat, do not give a flicker of remorse: being worshipped as a pseudo-god has just been too intoxicating. But sometimes we get the surprise of seeing genuine repentance and change. The Bible certainly shows plenty of all sides of this, from the stubborn refusal of Pharoah to give way, whatever the consequences (Exodus 5:1—14:31), through to the petty despotisms of the various members of the Herod family, from Herod the Great and his massacre of the innocents (Matthew 2:16–18), to other members of his family, such as the king responsible for the beheading of John the Baptist (see e.g. Matthew 2:22; Mark 6:14–29; Luke 19:12–27; Acts 12:1–4, 19–23). Yet the apostle Paul will not give up on the possibility that Herod Agrippa might after all become a Christian (Acts 26:27–29).

Who have we given up on? Are there certain individuals we know whom we have dismissed as incapable of change, or certain classes or groups of people? Paul – Saul of Tarsus – was certainly one of those that most Christians must have assumed was incapable of change (Acts 9:26–27), which is perhaps why he was never ready to give up, even on a member of the Herod family.

# 6 What is the shape of things to come?

**Acts 1:1–11**

Some science fiction is fantasy of the 'a long time ago in a galaxy far away' type; but much, like *Star Trek* and *Babylon 5*, pictures the future. In the case of *Star Trek*, this mythical future was a key part of its attraction because it was a hopeful future, where humanity had outgrown war and solved poverty, and sickness and disease readily succumbed to the wave of a medical tricorder (the fantasy gadget that diagnoses everything!).

What is the shape of things to come? Scripture holds two aspects in tension – clearly visible in Acts 1. The future remains to a degree unknown and unknowable. It is not for us 'to know the times or dates the Father has set' (v. 7) for the future. And yet this episode is full of future promises and prophecies: 'in a few days you will be baptised with the Holy Spirit' (v. 5); 'you will receive power' (v. 8); 'you will be my witnesses in Jerusalem, and in all Judea and Samaria, and to the ends of the earth' (v. 8); 'this same Jesus... will come back' (v. 11).

Fulfilment of prophecy is not the inexorable march of fate. Prophecy is not the same as prediction, as we see in Jonah. Jonah's prophecy of 'Forty days and Nineveh will be destroyed' (Jonah 3:4) was not followed by the city's destruction. Prophecy declares not immutable fate, but God's will – which is that Nineveh's people should repent (Jonah 3:10).

Biblical prophecy can thus operate as a divine warning; it can also provide comfort to the defeated (Isaiah 40:1–2). We should listen to prophets with discernment (1 Corinthians 14:29), and equally act on what we hear with discernment, as with Paul's unexpected response to the Spirit-given warning of Agabus and other prophets of his imminent arrest in Jerusalem (Acts 20:22–24; 21:4, 10–14).

But our ultimate future is that 'we shall see face to face' (1 Corinthians 13:12), and that 'we will all be changed' in the resurrection (1 Corinthians 15:51). The shape of things to come is determined by God, and our place within them determined by our relationship with God.

# Guidelines

Great drama, from the classics to contemporary forms like science fiction, provides a context in which to explore the great themes of life. Science fiction allows writers to tackle more directly some of the most fundamental issues in ways which conventional drama can't. So it raises questions about the nature of existence and reality, what defines our humanity – and what degrades it – and what our future might be.

Whether written by believers or unbelievers, the questions science fiction raises enable fruitful dialogue about the issues that matter to us as Christians. And as science fiction and fantasy are often very popular with teenagers and young adults, positive engagement with this genre can provide a context for creative conversations about the biggest issues of life with them.

As we reflect on the far-reaching issues raised this week, let us identify some of the questions we should also ask ourselves.

- How would you say your relationship with God affects your sense of being alone, or not alone?
- If advanced life on other planets was discovered, would that affect your faith? If so, how?
- Do you know what you want from life? Are you secure in answering the question 'Who are you?' Which question has the greater influence on the way you act?
- In an age of war and terrorism, do you understand those who despair that evil is unstoppable? How does the biblical revelation that God is ultimately in control help you?
- Is it too easy to give up on people who seem lost, and stop praying for them?
- How does thinking about our children's future affect you? And is our eternal future totally different, or connected?

---

**FURTHER READING**

Stephen May, *Stardust and Ashes: Science fiction in Christian perspective* (SPCK, 1998).

Anthony Thacker, *A Closer Look at Science Fiction* (Kingsway, 2001).

Anthony Thacker, *Behind the Sofa* (Kingsway, 2006).

*Overleaf... Guidelines* forthcoming issue | Author profile |
Recommended reading | Order and subscription forms

# *Guidelines* forthcoming issue

DAVID SPRIGGS

**At the heart of this issue we are celebrating the life-giving festival of Pentecost, when God poured out on the disciples his promised Holy Spirit and the church was launched on its Christ-appointed mission. This makes the writing of Jeremy Duff on the Spirit in Acts core to our biblical engagement. Jeremy will be exploring with us how the unfolding story of the life of the early church is in reality the story of the Holy Spirit guiding, empowering and blessing the obedience of those first Christians. It is a remarkable account and holds many clues and prompts for us as Christians today as we seek to live faithfully in a complex and ever changing culture.**

But whatever the culture, at the heart of our witness for Christ is the character which the Holy Spirit produces within us – indeed this aspect of the work of God's Spirit is about the personality of Jesus shining through us. Ian Macnair brings his biblical scholarship and pastoral experience to the well-known list of characteristics we call the fruit of the Spirit. He makes two fundamental points. First that this 'menu' is not a pick-and-mix one – we are called to allow God to grow them all in us. Secondly, as well as God's Spirit producing them, we need to pursue them. It is a shared responsibility!

Steve Motyer provides us with the narrative picture of Jesus to enrich and complement our understanding of who we are called to be as he continues his journey with Jesus in the early chapters of Mark's Gospel. We can glimpse a great deal about the heart of Jesus as we listen to his parables and as we see him not merely coping with but conquering the storm, demonic forces and biting criticism. All situations which require the fruit of the Spirit to handle as Jesus did.

Bishop Graham Dow shows us how the Bible can help us understand the demonic forces around us and how we can contribute to God's mission as he explores a variety of biblical passages on deliverance.

Ian Paul's exposition of 2 Timothy, Titus and Philemon shows how the fruit of the Spirit was no abstract moral list but was exemplified in the life of Paul and needed in the ongoing life of the churches.

Brian Howell's insights on the book of Genesis remind us that the development of the early church and its mission have an antecedent in the way God starts to form his people, the nation of Israel as his 'mission partner' to bring to fruition his purposes to redeem his broken creation. As with Acts, so with Genesis, we not only focus on individuals and their roles but are constantly reminded of the larger cultural context and the global vision of God.

Two other Old Testament contributions are Leviticus, in the capable hands of Fr Wansbrough, and the prophets Zephaniah and Habakkuk, which Brian is also writing. While Zephaniah seems to be a catalogue of the judgement of God on Israel and the nations, it also contains the amazing promise that he will remedy their rebellion and shameful deeds; he has taken away the judgement against them and will renew them in his love.

But for me the 'gem' of this issue is Mike Parsons' biblically-grounded insights on prayer through the lens of Calvin's thinking and practice.

May God equip us for every good work as we respond to his word.

# Author profile: Steve Motyer

**I was brought up believing that the scriptures are 'the final authority in all matters of faith and conduct', to quote the old UCCF Doctrinal Basis. Very Protestant! Whereas others believe that the church, or even human reason and science, intervene with an authority of their own, parallel to scripture, I've always been Protestant to the core. 'Sola Scriptura' was the Reformation summary of a principle that I hold dear: only scripture! – because the church must live its life under the authority of God himself, and not under any human authority. I love it, that the scriptures are this for us – the voice of God himself, addressing his world.**

There is something truly amazing about God's expression of himself in this particular 'word' to the world, the Bible: a random collection of stories, laws, prayers, prophecies, visions and proverbs packaged around the 1,500-year history of ancient Israel and of the Lord Jesus, Israel's Messiah, written in three different ancient languages. Because of this, the 'sola Scriptura' principle has a special shape, which means a lot to me: a shape given by the challenge of interpretation. How are we to interpret this scripture truly? – to hear its voice with clarity, the authentic voice of God himself? This teasing question has two poles to it, a 'then' and a 'now': how can we truly know what God meant to say then, to scripture's original speakers and hearers? And – on the back of that – how can we truly discern what God is saying to us now, by his Holy Spirit?

The Bible itself adds a further twist to these two questions. If this collection of various texts – this library of 66 very different writings – is the 'word' of one God, it must surely speak with one voice: but what is that single, unified message? Is it possible to discern and to state the core message that holds them all together, or underlies them all? As the many volumes devoted to this quest illustrate, it is possible that the unified message of the Bible – if it exists – must be expressed in words which actually appear nowhere within it. (Or is there a single text, somewhere in the Bible, which fully summarises the message of the whole?) The many volumes devoted to this quest also show that there is no agreement as to what that single summary of the Bible's message might be!

So here's the incredible truth, which for me sits at the heart of the gospel and of the Christian life I seek to live: God the Holy Spirit invites us to join a quest in which we dialogue with the scriptures and with each other about the meaning and impact of the Bible on our lives today, as we face into all the trials and joys that make up this amazing life. The Spirit invites us to share a journey on which we view scripture as our map and our guide – not like a satnav telling us where to turn next, but like a Dorling Kindersley *Eyewitness Travel Guide*, teasing us round the next corner with fascinating insights and illustrations, inviting us to go further, dig deeper, search more wisely, get stuck into this new culture with love and passion.

That's how the authority of scripture works for me: not like a rule book telling me what to think and do, but like a great teacher who stands alongside me as I learn, prodding me into new awareness, letting me fall over because when I get up I'll be better and stronger, providing a unparalleled learning experience. Spirit and Word go together! For me, the authority of scripture is an activity to pursue, not just a belief to hold.

This all became vividly real for me when I went through an emotional crisis and ended up training as a psychotherapist alongside my job teaching New Testament and Hermeneutics at London School of Theology. In obedience to God's call – and holding the scriptures in my hand – I ventured round this new corner and immersed myself in a whole new local culture. What richness! What discovery! Old doctrines suddenly took on more vibrant colours, and I began to see things in scripture that I could not have seen otherwise.

Because we're all so different, and on such different journeys, I think we'll never find an agreed statement of the 'core' message of the Bible. But the search will have been so worthwhile!

# Recommended reading

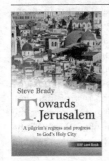

BRF's 2018 Lent book is by Steve Brady. *Towards Jerusalem* is a unique Lent book, a call to live for a vision bigger than ourselves, marching to a different drumbeat towards 'Zion', God's New Jerusalem and all that this means in transformative terms for today's Christian believer. The following extract is entitled 'A place for tears'.

Read Genesis 23:1–4 and 16–20.

Whether it comes through the windows, doors or sewers into the dwelling of our lives, death will arrive. Its statistics are most impressive; according to a quip by George Bernard Shaw, 'one out of one people die'. As I am writing this, I am trying to contact a relative whose husband woke up fighting for breath during the night, and was gone before the ambulance arrived. Every day in every generation, the great drama predicted back in Genesis is played out, 'dying you shall die' (2:17, literal translation).

Abraham may have been on his way to his promised land but his life's partner, Sarah, will not be there to enjoy it with him. Here's a lesser-known city we'll all visit sooner or later: Kiriath Arba. And some of us today are still raw with grief after visiting there with a loved one whom we had to leave behind, whether yesterday or years ago. Grief has many guises and disguises, and is as long as a piece of string. It is shortened or lengthened by many factors. How do we cope when Kiriath Arba beckons? May Abraham's example, with a few additions to it, turn us to the God who 'heals the broken-hearted and binds up their wounds' (Psalm 147:3).

## Be thankful

What a life Sarah and Abraham had shared. Sarah had set out with her husband on a journey of faith (Genesis 11:31) and, at 90, she'd given birth to a son (21:1–7). Like any life, it was not perfect, for neither was she. Her advice that Abram should sleep with her maid, Hagar, and the cruelty it subsequently provoked (16:1–16; 21:8–21) are not glossed over in the Bible. We are wise not to canonise in death our loved ones, as if they were perfect, even though they were wonderful to us.

## Be tearful

One of the positive elements to have entered our funeral culture in recent years is the note of celebration. What is concerning to some of us who conduct such events is that the bereaved are almost discouraged from grieving at all. In contrast, Abraham 'went to mourn for Sarah and to weep over her' (v. 2). This was not because he had no hope, or did not know about some form of life after death. Rather, as Paul reminds the Thessalonians, it was okay to grieve, but not 'like the rest of mankind, who have no hope' (1 Thessalonians 4:13). But we still grieve, because the Bible views death as an unlawful intruder who robs us of life. It is still 'the last enemy' (1 Corinthians 15:26), though it is not the last word – Christ is!

## Be resourceful

In death, there is a great deal to be done by the living, as this chapter amply demonstrates. Abraham needs to negotiate with Ephron the Hittite for a burial site. The oriental customs involved of bargaining over the price may mean Abraham paid 'over the odds' (vv. 10–16). On the other hand, we are acting wisely when we prepare in life for what we wish for in death. It has been my privilege to carry out, sometimes scrupulously, the wishes of the departed in terms of hymns chosen, things to say and passages to read. Thoughtful planning, clear communication and the valuing of the opportunity that one's funeral may present are to be commended.

## Be hopeful

It would be a mistake to see this chapter as an ancient version of how to preplan a funeral. Let's notice that the passage is topped and tailed by an electrifying word in its context: Canaan (vv. 2, 19). This is what Abraham's journeying is about. Although he is 'a foreigner and stranger' (v. 4), he now has a foothold and a grave in the promised land! It is not, to be sure, the holy city, but it is a marker of the promise of life. In laying Sarah's remains to rest, Abraham is anticipating the fulfilment of the promise of the one who says, 'a time is coming and has now come when the dead will hear the voice of the Son of God and those who hear will live', even those in the grave (John 5:25, 28). Christians are to face death, acknowledging both its pain and horror, while thanking God for Jesus, the resurrection and the life!

*To order a copy of this book, please turn to the order form on page 149.*

# Recommended reading

## Called by God
### Exploring our identity in Christ

**DEREK TIDBALL**
pb, 978 0 85746 530 6  £7.99

Who am I? It's a question many of us ask ourselves at some point in life. In this fascinating book, Derek Tidball explores finding who God is calling us to be and what he is calling us to do. He explores twelve key New Testament texts which speak of the Christian's calling. In a time when we can get lost in the quest for identity, this book brings us back to the Bible and to Christ at the centre of it all.

## The Recovery of Joy
### Finding the path from rootlessness to returning home

**NAOMI STARKEY**
pb, 978 0 85746 518 4  £6.99

Naomi Starkey weaves imaginative stories with profound biblical reflections on several of the psalms to trace a journey that many of us will relate to. The narrative begins in rootlessness and despair, and takes the reader across the sea to a series of islands. These are the settings for a sequence of events and encounters through which we can progress from that initial rootlessness, through healing, to a rediscovery of the joy of feeling at the centre of God's loving purpose for our lives.

# Engaging the Word
## Biblical literacy and Christian discipleship

**PETER M. PHILLIPS**
pb, 978 0 85746 583 2  £7.99

Peter Phillips is convinced that the church in the West is not devouring the Bible; it's not meditating on the word as it should. *Engaging the Word* will transform the Bible engagement habits of Christian disciples and leaders. It will make an impact on the spiritual health of the church – opening new opportunities for drawing on God's word and new life as a result. A series of practical explorations of the role of the Bible will help readers reach up to God, reach in to develop understanding of identity in Christ and reach out to others.

# Jesus through the Old Testament
## Transform your Bible understanding

**GRAEME GOLDSWORTHY**
pb, 978 0 85746 567 2  £7.99

Confident in the Old Testament?

Enjoying reading it?

Happy to preach from it?

In this engaging book, Graeme Goldsworthy reflects with clarity and practical insight on reading and using the Old Testament. By showing us how Jesus is central to the Old Testament's message, he encourages us to reinstate it as essential and transformative to our lives, churches and mission in today's world. The author asks important questions: Where is Jesus in the whole biblical storyline? How does the kingdom of God relate to him? In what way is he central to the divine revelation? This is a must-read for those who wish to transform their biblical understanding.

line: **brfonline.org.uk**
ephone: +44 (0)1865 319700
n–Fri 9.15–17.30

Delivery times within the UK are normally
15 working days. Prices are correct at the time of
going to press but may change without prior notice.

| itle | Price | Qty | Total |
|---|---|---|---|
| owards Jerusalem | £7.99 | | |
| alled by God | £7.99 | | |
| he Recovery of Joy | £6.99 | | |
| ngaging the Word | £7.99 | | |
| esus through the Old Testament | £7.99 | | |
| iving the Prayer | £7.99 | | |

| POSTAGE AND PACKING CHARGES | | | |
|---|---|---|---|
| der value | UK | Europe | Rest of world |
| der £7.00 | £2.00 | £5.00 | £7.00 |
| 00–£29.99 | £3.00 | £9.00 | £15.00 |
| 0.00 and over | FREE | £9.00 + 15% of order value | £15.00 + 20% of order value |

| Total value of books | |
|---|---|
| Postage and packing | |
| **Total for this order** | |

ase complete in **BLOCK CAPITALS**

itle ............ First name/initials ..................... Surname.................................................

Address...................................................................................................................

..................................................................................... Postcode ......................

cc. No. ........................................ Telephone .....................................................

mail.......................................................................................................................

Please keep me informed about BRF's books and resources ❏ by email ❏ by post
Please keep me informed about the wider work of BRF ❏ by email ❏ by post

## Method of payment

❏ Cheque (made payable to BRF)   ❏ MasterCard / Visa

Card no. ☐☐☐☐ ☐☐☐☐ ☐☐☐☐ ☐☐☐☐

alid from [M][M] [Y][Y]   Expires [M][M] [Y][Y]   Security code* ☐☐☐
Last 3 digits on the reverse of the card

ignature* ......................................................................... Date ........... /........... /...........
ESSENTIAL IN ORDER TO PROCESS YOUR ORDER

ase **return this form to:** BRF, 15 The Chambers, Vineyard, Abingdon OX14 3FE | enquiries@brf.org.uk
ead our terms and find out about cancelling your order, please visit **brfonline.org.uk/terms**.

The Bible Reading Fellowship (BRF) is a Registered Charity (233280)

# How to encourage Bible reading in your church

BRF has been helping individuals connect with the Bible for over 90 years. We want to support churches as they seek to encourage church members into regular Bible reading.

### Order a Bible reading resources pack

This pack is designed to give your church the tools to publicise our Bible reading notes. It includes:

- Sample Bible reading notes for your congregation to try.
- Publicity resources, including a poster.
- A church magazine feature about Bible reading notes.

The pack is free, but we welcome a £5 donation to cover the cost of postage. If you require a pack to be sent outside the UK or require a specific number of sample Bible reading notes, please contact us for postage costs. More information about what the current pack contains is available on our website.

### How to order and find out more

- Visit **biblereadingnotes.org.uk/for-churches**
- Telephone BRF on +44 (0)1865 319700 Mon–Fri 9.15–17.30
- Write to us at BRF, 15 The Chambers, Vineyard, Abingdon OX14 3FE

### Keep informed about our latest initiatives

We are continuing to develop resources to help churches encourage people into regular Bible reading, wherever they are on their journey. Join our email list at **biblereadingnotes.org.uk/helpingchurches** to stay informed about the latest initiatives that your church could benefit from.

### Introduce a friend to our notes

We can send information about our notes and current prices for you to pass on. Please contact us.

# Transforming lives and communities

BRF is a charity that is passionate about making a difference through the Christian faith. We want to see lives and communities transformed through our creative programmes and resources for individuals, churches and schools. We are doing this by resourcing:

- **Christian growth and understanding of the Bible.** Through our Bible reading notes, books, digital resources, Quiet Days and other events, we're resourcing individuals, groups and leaders in churches for their own spiritual journey and for their ministry.

- **Church outreach in the local community.** BRF is the home of three programmes that churches are embracing to great effect as they seek to engage with their local communities: Messy Church, Who Let The Dads Out? and The Gift of Years.

- **Teaching Christianity in primary schools.** Our Barnabas in Schools team is working with primary-aged children and their teachers, enabling them to explore Christianity creatively and confidently within the school curriculum.

- **Children's and family ministry.** Through our Parenting for Faith programme, websites and published resources, we're working with churches and families, enabling children and adults alike to explore Christianity creatively and bring the Bible alive.

## Do you share our vision?

Sales of our books and Bible reading notes cover the cost of producing them. However, our other programmes are funded primarily by donations, grants and legacies. If you share our vision, would you help us to transform even more lives and communities? Your prayers and financial support are vital for the work that we do.

- You could support BRF's ministry with a one-off gift or regular donation (using the response form on page 153).

- You could consider making a bequest to BRF in your will (page 152).

- You could encourage your church to support BRF as part of your church's giving to home mission – perhaps focusing on a specific area of our ministry, or a particular member of our Barnabas in Schools team.

- Most important of all, you could support BRF with your prayers.

# Make a lasting difference through a gift in your will

BRF's story began in 1922 when a vicar in Brixton, south London, introduced daily Bible readings to help his congregation 'get a move on spiritually'. Over the coming years, several other churches joined the scheme and more and more copies of the Bible reading notes were printed. By 1939 an amazing 238,000 copies were being printed and read.

The past 90 years have certainly seen BRF flourish. We still produce and distribute Bible reading notes, but our work now encompasses so much more and its impact stretches across the globe, from Brixton to Brisbane.

Today we are the home of creative programmes like Messy Church, which reaches an estimated 500,000 people each month. We encourage churches to reach out to fathers through Who Let The Dads Out? and we help meet the spiritual needs of older people through The Gift of Years. We also enable primary schools to teach Christianity creatively within the curriculum, and equip parents to effectively disciple their children through Parenting for Faith. At the heart of it all is a desire to help children and adults of all ages explore Christianity and grow in faith.

If you share our passion for making a difference through the Christian faith, please consider leaving a gift in your will to BRF. Gifts in wills are an important source of income for us and they don't need to be huge to make a real difference. For every £1 we receive we invest 95p back into charitable activities. Just imagine what we could do over the next century with your help.

For further information about making a gift to BRF in your will, please visit **brf.org.uk/lastingdifference**, contact Sophie Aldred on **01865 319700** or email **giving@brf.org.uk**.

**Whatever you can do or give, we thank you for your support**.

## SHARING OUR VISION – MAKING A GIFT

**I would like to make a gift to support BRF. Please use my gift for:**

☐ where it is needed most ☐ Barnabas Children's Ministry

☐ Messy Church ☐ Who Let The Dads Out? ☐ The Gift of Years

| Title | First name/initials | Surname |
|-------|---------------------|---------|
| Address | | |
| | | Postcode |
| Email | | |
| Telephone | | |
| Signature | | Date |

*giftaid it*  You can add an extra 25p to every £1 you give.

**Please treat as Gift Aid donations all qualifying gifts of money made**

☐ today, ☐ in the past four years, ☐ and in the future.

I am a UK taxpayer and understand that if I pay less Income Tax and/or Capital Gains Tax in the current tax year than the amount of Gift Aid claimed on all my donations, it is my responsibility to pay any difference.

☐ My donation does not qualify for Gift Aid.

Please notify BRF if you want to cancel this Gift Aid declaration, change your name or home address, or no longer pay sufficient tax on your income and/or capital gains.

Please complete other side of form ➡

**Please return this form to:**
BRF, 15 The Chambers, Vineyard, Abingdon OX14 3FE

**BRF**

The Bible Reading Fellowship is a Registered Charity (233280)

## SHARING OUR VISION – MAKING A GIFT

### Regular giving

**By Direct Debit:**

☐ I would like to make a regular gift of £ [     ] per month/quarter/year.
Please also complete the Direct Debit instruction on page 159.

**By Standing Order:**

Please contact Priscilla Kew  +44 (0)1235 462305 | giving@brf.org.uk

### One-off donation

**Please accept my gift of:**

☐ £10  ☐ £50  ☐ £100  Other £ [     ]

by (delete as appropriate):

☐ Cheque/Charity Voucher payable to 'BRF'

☐ MasterCard/Visa/Debit card/Charity card

Name on card

Card no. [ ][ ][ ][ ] [ ][ ][ ][ ] [ ][ ][ ][ ] [ ][ ][ ][ ]

Valid from [M][M] [Y][Y]  Expires [M][M] [Y][Y]

Security code* [ ][ ][ ]  *Last 3 digits on the reverse of the card
ESSENTIAL IN ORDER TO PROCESS YOUR PAYMENT

Signature                                    Date

We like to acknowledge all donations. However, if you do not wish to receive
an acknowledgement, please tick here ☐

⬅ Please complete other side of form

**Please return this form to:**
BRF, 15 The Chambers, Vineyard, Abingdon OX14 3FE

The Bible Reading Fellowship is a Registered Charity (233280)

GL0118

## GUIDELINES SUBSCRIPTION RATES

Please note our new subscription rates, current until 30 April 2019:

**Individual subscriptions**
covering 3 issues for under 5 copies, payable in advance
(including postage & packing):

|  | UK | Europe | Rest of world |
|---|---|---|---|
| *Guidelines* 1-year subscription | £16.95 | £25.20 | £29.10 |
| *Guidelines* 3-year subscription (9 issues) | £46.35 | N/A | N/A |

**Group subscriptions**
covering 3 issues for 5 copies or more, sent to **one** UK address (post free):

| | |
|---|---|
| *Guidelines* 1-year subscription | £13.50 per set of 3 issues p.a. |

Please note that the annual billing period for group subscriptions runs from 1 May to 30 April.

**Overseas group subscription rates**
Available on request. Please email **enquiries@brf.org.uk**.

Copies may also be obtained from Christian bookshops:

| | |
|---|---|
| *Guidelines* | £4.50 per copy |

---

All our Bible reading notes can be ordered online by visiting
**biblereadingnotes.org.uk/subscriptions**

For information about our other Bible reading notes,
and apps for iPhone and iPod touch, visit
**biblereadingnotes.org.uk**

---

## GUIDELINES INDIVIDUAL SUBSCRIPTION FORM

All our Bible reading notes can be ordered online by visiting
**biblereadingnotes.org.uk/subscriptions**

☐ I would like to take out a subscription:

Title ............. First name/initials ................. Surname ..........................................

Address ........................................................................................................

........................................................... Postcode .....................

Telephone ........................... Email ..........................................................

Please send *Guidelines* beginning with the May 2018 / September 2018 / January 2019 issue (*delete as appropriate*):

| (*please tick box*) | UK | Europe | Rest of world |
|---|---|---|---|
| *Guidelines* 1-year subscription | ☐ £16.95 | ☐ £25.20 | ☐ £29.10 |
| *Guidelines* 3-year subscription | ☐ £46.35 | N/A | N/A |

Total enclosed £ ..................... (cheques should be made payable to 'BRF')

Please charge my MasterCard / Visa ☐ Debit card ☐ with £ ..................

Card no. ☐☐☐☐ ☐☐☐☐ ☐☐☐☐ ☐☐☐☐

Valid from ☐☐☐☐ Expires ☐☐☐☐ Security code* ☐☐☐

Last 3 digits on the reverse of the card

Signature* ................................................................. Date ....... / ....... / .......

*ESSENTIAL IN ORDER TO PROCESS YOUR PAYMENT

To set up a Direct Debit, please also complete the Direct Debit instruction on page 159 and return it to BRF with this form.

**Please return this form with the appropriate payment to:**
BRF, 15 The Chambers, Vineyard, Abingdon OX14 3FE

To read our terms and find out about cancelling your order, please visit **brfonline.org.uk/terms**.

The Bible Reading Fellowship (BRF) is a Registered Charity (233280)

GL0118

## GUIDELINES GIFT SUBSCRIPTION FORM

☐ I would like to give a gift subscription (please provide both names and addresses):

Title ............. First name/initials ................ Surname ....................................

Address ............................................................................................

.................................................................. Postcode ...........................

Telephone .............................. Email ...................................................

Gift subscription name .........................................................................

Gift subscription address ......................................................................

.................................................................. Postcode ...........................

Gift message (20 words max. or include your own gift card):

....................................................................................................

....................................................................................................

Please send *Guidelines* beginning with the May 2018 / September 2018 / January 2019 issue (*delete as appropriate*):

| (please tick box) | UK | Europe | Rest of world |
|---|---|---|---|
| *Guidelines* 1-year subscription | ☐ £16.95 | ☐ £25.20 | ☐ £29.10 |
| *Guidelines* 3-year subscription | ☐ £46.35 | N/A | N/A |

Total enclosed £ ..................... (cheques should be made payable to 'BRF')

Please charge my MasterCard / Visa ☐ Debit card ☐ with £ ................

Card no. ☐☐☐☐ ☐☐☐☐ ☐☐☐☐ ☐☐☐☐

Valid from ☐☐☐☐ Expires ☐☐☐☐ Security code* ☐☐☐
Last 3 digits on the reverse of the card

Signature* ........................................................... Date ....../....../......

*ESSENTIAL IN ORDER TO PROCESS YOUR PAYMENT

To set up a Direct Debit, please also complete the Direct Debit instruction on page 159 and return it to BRF with this form.

**Please return this form with the appropriate payment to:**
BRF, 15 The Chambers, Vineyard, Abingdon OX14 3FE

To read our terms and find out about cancelling your order, please visit **brfonline.org.uk/terms**.

The Bible Reading Fellowship (BRF) is a Registered Charity (233280)

## DIRECT DEBIT PAYMENT

You can pay for your annual subscription to our Bible reading notes using Direct Debit. You need only give your bank details once, and the payment is made automatically every year until you cancel it. If you would like to pay by Direct Debit, please use the form opposite, entering your BRF account number under 'Reference number'.

You are fully covered by the Direct Debit Guarantee:

### The Direct Debit Guarantee

- This Guarantee is offered by all banks and building societies that accept instructions to pay Direct Debits.

- If there are any changes to the amount, date or frequency of your Direct Debit, The Bible Reading Fellowship will notify you 10 working days in advance of your account being debited or as otherwise agreed. If you request The Bible Reading Fellowship to collect a payment, confirmation of the amount and date will be given to you at the time of the request.

- If an error is made in the payment of your Direct Debit, by The Bible Reading Fellowship or your bank or building society, you are entitled to a full and immediate refund of the amount paid from your bank or building society.

- If you receive a refund you are not entitled to, you must pay it back when The Bible Reading Fellowship asks you to.

- You can cancel a Direct Debit at any time by simply contacting your bank or building society. Written confirmation may be required. Please also notify us.

GL0118

The Bible Reading Fellowship

# Instruction to your bank or building society to pay by Direct Debit

Please fill in the whole form using a ballpoint pen and return it to:
BRF, 15 The Chambers, Vineyard, Abingdon OX14 3FE

Service User Number: | 5 | 5 | 8 | 2 | 2 | 9 |

Name and full postal address of your bank or building society

| To: The Manager | Bank/Building Society |
|---|---|
| Address | |
| | |
| | |
| | Postcode |

Name(s) of account holder(s)

| |
|---|

Branch sort code

| | | – | | | – | | |

Bank/Building Society account number

| | | | | | | | | |

Reference number

| | | | | | | |

**Instruction to your Bank/Building Society**
Please pay The Bible Reading Fellowship Direct Debits from the account detailed in this instruction, subject to the safeguards assured by the Direct Debit Guarantee. I understand that this instruction may remain with The Bible Reading Fellowship and, if so, details will be passed electronically to my bank/building society.

| Signature(s) |
|---|
| |

Banks and Building Societies may not accept Direct Debit instructions for some types of account.